BIRDING FOR
THE AMATEUR NATURALIST

"This small book is written in conversational style and, with its accompanying charts and illustrations, offers much valuable information for the first-time birder, as well as the seasoned naturalist."
—*Dallas Morning News*

"Entertaining and informative."
—*Chattanooga* (TN) *Times*

"One of the best basic bird-watcher's books to come out in some time ... A concise handbook for amateur bird watchers containing helpful information on technique, equipment, and special projects."
—*A.L.A. Booklist*

"Beyond the backyard feeder there are important research projects that are fascinating and fun to do."
—*Bookazine Bulletin*

"Beginning bird watchers will find a wealth of information."
—*North American Bird Bander*

BIRDING FOR
THE AMATEUR NATURALIST

_____

Laura O'Biso Socha

Illustrated by Dominique Paulus-Warner

An East Woods Book

The
Globe
Pequot
Press

Chester, Connecticut

Published 1989 by The Globe Pequot Press
© 1987 by Laura O'Biso Socha

Library of Congress Cataloging-in-Publication Data

Socha, Laura O' Biso.
  Birding for the amateur naturalist / Laura O'Biso Socha; illustrated by
Dominique Paulus.
—1st ed.
    p. cm.
  Reprint. Originally published: 1st ed. New York, N.Y. : Dodd, Mead, c1987
  Includes bibliographies and index.
  ISBN 0–87106–615–7
  1. Bird watching. 2. Ornithology—Field work. I. Title.
[QL677.5.S63 1989]
598'.07'234—dc19   88–34648
                                                              CIP

Manufactured in the United States of America
First Edition/Third Printing

For Mom and Daddy

Thank you for having the wisdom to raise your children in the country and for allowing us to grow with freedom of thought and expression, guided by love.

CONTENTS

ACKNOWLEDGMENTS

A book is never written by the author alone. I want to thank all of the people that helped me through this project with their support, suggestions, and cooperation, especially: Dot Hughes and the crew at Raccoon Ridge Bird Observatory for their patience and understanding; Dominique Paulus-Warner for the hours she spent creating the illustrations; my son, Rob, for always believing in me no matter what; and Carol Valotta for helping me through some difficult times. Thanks also to everyone who responded to my inquiries and to the editors and staff at The Globe Pequot Press for their combined talents, professional manner, and genuine concern.

PREFACE

Few people ever sit down and plan to become birders. It is usually a gradual process, sparked by some special observation or occurrence that sticks in your mind, becoming the foundation for a whole new way of looking at things, especially birds.

I can remember the special incident that sparked such an interest in me. I was about ten, sent out to the clothesline to retrieve my brother's favorite pair of well-worn bluejeans. But there was something awkward about the jeans; and as I approached the clothesline, I discovered that a pair of house wrens had selected the right leg of the jeans as the perfect place to build a nest. Using the hole at the knee as their entrance (and in the space of a few hours' drying time), the birds had stuffed the leg so completely with twigs that the denim was nearly bursting at the seams. The woody material was woven and packed so tightly that none of it could slip out the bottom of the pant leg.

The house wren was one of my father's favorite birds, and he promptly declared the jeans off-limits to my brother . . . at least until nesting season was over. Lacking the faith in the jeans that the wrens seemed to have, we pinned the bottom of the leg securely. I followed the progress of three successful broods in those jeans that year. From that summer on, simply watching was not enough.

And that is where the best birding really begins—when you are no longer contented with simply *seeing* a bird.

This book is for those "bird watchers" who are ready to do more than "watch"—even if it is only for personal fulfillment, though as you will see, amateurs should never underestimate the value of their work. People have been watching birds for thousands of years, yet we are still scratching the surface of all there is to know.

Birding can be enjoyed alone or with others, full time or whenever you get the chance, with little equipment or with the whole collection on the market. This book is not intended to be a scientific textbook on ornithology. It is intended to provide gentle encouragement to the person who would like to expand his or her interest in birds beyond simple identification and to expose that person to a sampling of the endless possibilities that exist for amateur naturalists.

The book draws largely upon my personal experiences as an eager observer in the field and upon my experiences as a bird bander and rehabilitator. I hope that, through reading this book, you will gain the incentive and the confidence to explore your interest in birds and the extra measure of peace and enjoyment in your life that birding will bring.

THE SCIENCE
OF WATCHING BIRDS

Backyard Naturalist Ltd
156 main
Unionville 513-9214

WildernessFeeds Dstr
115 TORBAY
Markham 9409060

Birders Natur Store
265 EglintonW
416 481 2431

Earth + Sky
50 Bloor W - Lower Conc
Holt Renfrew Centre
416 968 2665

The Science
of Watching Birds

Bird Watcher. Just mention the term and your mind conjures up an image of an eccentric, absent-minded character dressed in khaki shorts and hiking boots, juggling binoculars, field guides, notebooks, and assorted paraphernalia while slogging through a swamp at four in the morning in hot pursuit of the "purple-breasted, yellow-tailed, orange-eyed dickeybird."

But everyone, to a certain extent, is a bird watcher. It cannot be helped. Birds are among the most abundant, and certainly are the most obvious, of all wild creatures, easily observed living, feeding, and raising their young in close proximity to humans, in any habitat, during any season. Bird watching, in its simplest form, is little more than acknowledging the presence of a particular bird.

But what happens when you want to know more about the birds you are seeing? How will you answer all the questions that will naturally occur to you? What kind of bird is that? What is it doing? I wonder what it eats. Why is it singing like that? Where does it go in the winter? How does it find its way? Where does it raise its young? Here . . . in my backyard? I never noticed!

Once you begin to ask questions, you have really started bird watching. It sounds the same, it is spelled the same, but it represents a new outlook about birds in particular, and wildlife in general. Now you're thinking like an ornithologist.

Today, the scientific study of birds is based on bird *watching*. While early ornithologists "watched" birds using a shotgun instead of binoculars, and learned by studying the bodies of species they had collected, modern ornithologists are more concerned with the everyday life of the living bird. Most of the initial discovery, collection, identification, and naming of each species has been accomplished, except for new species occasionally discovered in the more remote areas of the world. We already know the basic anatomy and physiology of birds—how they fly, why they lay eggs, and how and why they grow feathers. What we are still investigating are a million mysteries about their daily lives. How do they live from day to day? How do they manage to travel halfway around the world and return to the same tree without benefit of map or motor? How do they know which way to go? Which way *do* they go? Why do they migrate, and how do they know when it is time to leave or return? How does a bird instinctively know where and when and how to build a nest? What factors determine a bird's chosen habitat? These are just a few questions that come to mind.

Some of these questions may never be fully answered. Some answers lead only to more questions. But the study of birdlife centers on one thing—observation. If you are a keen observer, you can be a bona fide ornithologist.

The science of watching birds does not require the college degree or technical background so vital in most other scientific fields. Within birding circles, degrees and titles are no match for pure interest, enthusiasm, and talent for observation. Any amateur bird watcher can achieve success, personal satisfaction, "professional" status, peer recognition, and even a little fame and fortune for his or her birding efforts.

Most of the ornithological information we have today is the direct result of contributions made by amateur bird watchers and naturalists. Many works considered classic references by today's birders are the efforts of amateur naturalists. Margaret Morse Nice, a housewife with several children, researched and wrote her *Studies in the Life History of the Song Sparrow* in her spare time. Arthur Cleveland Bent, a "frail youth" with boundless energy, became a successful businessman who studied birds in his spare time; the Dover editions of his world-famous series of life histories should be in every birder's personal library. Amateur naturalists are the lifeblood of ornithology, and without their efforts and contributions, our knowledge of birds might still be in the dark ages.

Actually, there are many terms used to describe bird watchers. The semantics and explanations can be amusing, however, and should be taken lightly. It is generally understood that a "bird watcher" is someone who watches birds for pleasure, while a "birder" is more intense and scientific. Yet others seem to think that a bird watcher is the one who really studies the birds, while the birder is more of a competitive lister. Then there are the professionals and the amateurs, though no one is sure where the two are separated, if they can be, since those who call themselves amateurs often know more than some professionals.

A recent seminar of amateur and professional ornithologists pondered this subject for some time, and reached the accepted conclusion that a person earning a living from his or her work with birds should be called a professional, while all others were amateurs, so that money, not knowledge, became the distinguishing factor. In this book, however, terms will be applied loosely and may be used interchangeably.

As mentioned above, the most important factors are a genuine interest and enthusiasm and skills for keen observation. The first must be generated within yourself; the latter can be learned and will improve with practice. Start with the basics, one step at a time, and everything else will fall into place.

BIRDING BASICS

To a beginning birder, having the ability to identify all of those confusing birds seems like nothing short of sheer genius. How can you possibly pick an individual species out of a flock of brown-striped sparrows that all look the same? How do you identify a bird when all you see is a silhouette against the clouds? How can you distinguish one species from another as you watch dozens of little shorebirds running in a crowd up and down the beach?

First, relax. Learning to identify birds is no more difficult

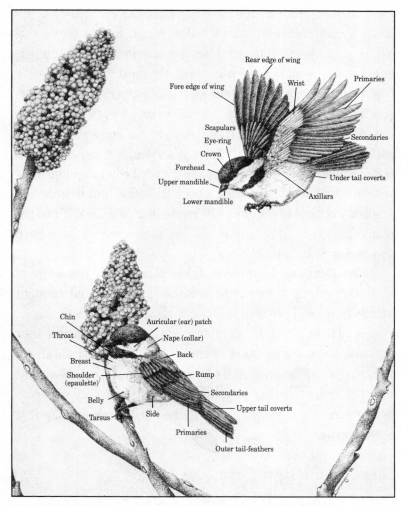

These anatomical terms are used for identifying birds in the field.

than learning to identify anything else you see. How do you know a cocker spaniel from a collie? A lion from a house cat? Think about what happens when you are introduced to a person you have never seen before. Your mind immediately begins to take notes about the physical appearance of the person before you: size, shape, form, color of eyes, skin, hair, unique features, dress, and so forth. As you engage in conversation, you are aware of the person's voice, manner of speech, command of the language, gestures, and "body language"—all without consciously thinking about it. Individual details will instantly coalesce, and you will remember (the face, if not the name) and recognize this person as someone you have seen and talked to before.

The same mental process takes place when you attempt to identify birds. If you approach the task with that thought in mind, you will see that it is not such an impossible feat.

Birds, like people, display certain physical traits that separate them from others of their kind. The same details of size, shape, form, color, body language, voice, and movement will also come together to form a distinctive picture of a particular bird. Once you have learned what to look for, the rest comes easily.

Basic Identification Techniques

One of the best places to begin the study of identification is within the pages of a good field guide; but do not try to memorize the whole book! Start small, concentrating on a few of the most common birds for your area. (If you are not sure what these are, your local bird club, Audubon Society chapter, or area nature center can provide you with the information.) Many organizations recommend that beginners try to get out into the field with an experienced birder, and by all means this is helpful. But, if you do not know any experienced birders who can help you, don't be afraid to go it alone. Birding in general, and field identification in particular, is a learning experience, even for the most seasoned observer.

SHAPE. The shape of the bird is one of the most important clues to its identity. To an experienced eye, the shape or silhouette of a bird is often enough to identify it (many migrating hawks are identified by their shape). Differences in shape can also be effective in separating similar species. Again as an example, migrating Cooper's hawks can usually be distinguished from the similar sharp-shinned hawk by the shape of the tail—rounded tip in the Cooper's and squared tip in the sharpie.

SIZE. Although the size of a particular bird is a physical characteristic that does not change, it may easily be distorted by lighting and distance, so that the bird may appear larger or smaller than it actually is. In spite of this distortion, determining the size of the bird you are observing can be very helpful in separating similar species. Try to relate the size to a bird that you know. Is it smaller than a robin, larger than a crow? If you find it difficult to compare the bird to a bird you are familiar with, try to relate it to something in the bird's immediate vicinity, such as the leaves on the trees.

COLOR. Color is the one thing many people think about first, yet as an identification aid it is one of the least reliable

a. Kingfisher
b. Hawk-like
c. Owl
d. Merganser
e. Duck
f. Goose
g. Gull
h. Sandpiper
i. Loon
j. Tern
k. Ibis
l. Heron

m. Finch
n. Warbler
o. Sparrow
p. Chickadee
q. Woodpecker
r. Wren
s. Chicken-like
t. Waxwing
u. Thrush
v. Grosbeak
w. Dove
x. Crow-like

---

1. Herring Gull
2. Red-tailed Hawk
3. Bald Eagle
4. Turkey Vulture
5. Vireo
6. Wren
7. Sparrow
8. Kingbird
9. Swallow
10. Crow
11. Mourning Dove
12. Blue Jay
13. Robin
14. Great Horned Owl
15. Cedar Waxwing
16. Flycatcher
17. Kingfisher
18. Yellow-shafted Flicker

19. Horned Lark
20. Mockingbird
21. Finch
22. Warbler
23. Bluebird
24. Chickadee
25. Nuthatch
26. Quail
27. Pheasant
28. Turkey
29. Killdeer
30. Canada Goose
31. Ruffed Grouse
32. Great Blue Heron
33. Ibis
34. Mallard
35. Mute Swan

under any but perfect conditions. The amount and direction of available light can transform the most brilliantly colored species to a dull, shadowy image (here is where shape, size, and behavior become so important). This is particularly true of warblers observed high in the trees, backlit by the sky. It is almost impossible to distinguish colors under those circumstances.

FIELD MARKS. Field marks (also called flash marks) will come to the rescue when colors fail you, for even in poor lighting you will be able to detect these striking color patterns. Some are visible when the bird is stationary, but most are more easily observed as the bird flies. Many are diagnostic: the white rump and yellow feather shafts of the flicker as it flies away from you, the orange wing and tail patches of the male redstart. A dark-eyed junco might easily be confused with flocking sparrows, but when the bird flies, the white outer tail feathers "flash" junco!

BEHAVIOR. Observing the behavior of birds is probably the most important key to learning their identity. It is by far the most interesting, and it is the foundation on which nearly all other studies are based. By observing what a bird is doing—and this encompasses virtually every move the bird makes (or doesn't make)—very often you can either place the bird in the proper family group or identify it outright. As an example: woodpeckers, nuthatches, and creepers might be confusing to a beginning birder. They appear to be legless birds with sharply pointed beaks, usually observed going up and down the trunk of a tree. But, a simple difference in the *manner* in which the birds go up and down separates the three groups. Woodpeckers usually "hitch" up the trunk of the tree and "back" down tail first. Nuthatches will also hitch up the tree, but they will turn around and come down headfirst. Creepers begin at the bottom, work their way up spiral-fashion, then fly to the base of the next tree.

FAMILY GROUP. This step towards identification is often overlooked by beginning birders, yet it will go a long way to avoid confusion and, if nothing else, tell you in what section of the field guide you should be looking! If you know you are observing a member of the thrush family, or a warbler, or a flycatcher, or a heron, the route to identifying the individual bird will become much easier.

HABITAT. All birds will naturally seek out their preferred habitats. Knowing what species you are most likely to find in any given area can enhance your birding experiences and make identification easier. Sometimes the knowledge of a species' habitat requirement may be the only clue you have to separate it from seemingly identical birds. The classic examples are the three flycatchers that, even to the most experienced birder, look alike in the field. They can be identified more readily by their habitat preferences: the least flycatcher in dry, open woods; the alder flycatcher in wet marshy areas; and the Acadian flycatcher in moist woods.

SONG. It takes a bit longer to develop an ear for the song of a bird, but when you can identify the presence of a particular species just by hearing it sing, it is like being the honored guest at a command performance. It is a skill that requires patience, a good ear, a better memory, and practice, practice,

practice. Start small, with a few species, and *try to observe the bird as it is singing*. This will go a long way toward connecting the song with a particular bird in your mind. There are many good-quality recordings available to help with this task. See the list of recommended references for information.

Basic Birding Equipment

The serious birder needs only a pair of binoculars and a good field guide to pursue an interest. This is not to say you cannot or will not spend a small fortune on the staggering array of equipment available to birders today—just keep in mind that most of these things are optional.

BINOCULARS. These are by far the most important piece of equipment you will need. Binoculars vary tremendously in size, weight, brightness of image, field of view, lenses, lens coatings, and magnification. Top-of-the-line models may cost hundreds or thousands of dollars. Choosing binoculars that are right for you and your needs is most important, since binoculars tend to become very personal tools. Once you have a favorite pair, you will find that using another will seem awkward.

Most birders prefer 7 x 35s for general use. Keep in mind that the higher the magnification, the more difficult it will be to keep things in focus, since you are also magnifying your movements. Take your time with your selection, and buy the best pair you can afford. You will depend on your binoculars, and the wrong pair will interfere with rather than enhance your birding experiences.

FIELD GUIDES. The birder's bible! There are many fine guides available today, and, if you acquire the birding habit, you will probably own them all eventually. The beginner should choose a book that illustrates males, females, and immatures and offers illustrations of birds in different seasonal plumages. The newer guides that offer photographs of particular species are very helpful, but not necessarily when you are in need of that initial identification, since the photograph may not show all that you need to see. It can, however, confirm your guess after you have found the bird in your artist-illustrated guide. Two of the best guides on the market are Roger Tory Peterson's *Field Guide to the Birds of North America* and the Golden Press *Birds of North America* by Chandler Robbins, Bertel Bruun, and Herbert Zim. Both books have been revised and updated recently.

Among the guides offering photographs of birds, I prefer the three volumes of *The Audubon Society Master Guide to Birding*. Most of the photographs in this series are of very high quality, and the books also offer identification tips for males, females, immatures, and seasonal plumages.

NOTEBOOKS AND JOURNALS. Next to your binoculars and field guides, a notebook and a journal may be the only other necessities for enjoyable and productive birding. Some birders prefer to keep two. They take a pocket-sized spiral pad into the field; when they return from a birding trip, they transcribe their notes into a larger volume. Although there is a danger that something might be lost in transcribing, more than likely you will be able to handle that, and you may find yourself adding to your notes as you remember the events of the day in a more relaxed atmosphere.

RECORDING WHAT YOU SEE. More important than what type of notebook or journal you use is what you put into it. You may want to jot down a few key words or phrases, or you may ramble on for pages. Whatever method you use, there are a few things to keep in mind. First, get into the habit of recording what you see as soon as possible. Do not tell yourself you will remember everything when you get home and that you will write it all out later. You won't. Making consistent entries in your field journal may very well be the most difficult part of your birding habit. It requires self-discipline and some extra work, but the rewards are certainly worth the effort. Any serious study of birds cannot occur without written records. When you are making entries, remember to write legibly! There is nothing worse than looking back at your notes a week later and being unable to understand what you have written.

Some birders prefer to divide their journals into sections; one for general observations, another for notes on individual species. Regardless of the record-keeping method you favor, a good journal entry should include the date, the names of everyone on the particular outing, the time of the sighting, notations on the weather conditions (temperature, wind direction and velocity, and so on), a detailed description of the bird (especially if identification is shaky), what the bird is doing, and the approximate length of time the bird is observed. Include the location of the sighting, the lighting and visibility conditions, your distance from the bird, and anything else that seems important at the moment. If this sounds like a lot to be recording while you are frantically trying to see the bird in the first place, you are right. But, the more you do it, the easier it will become. The only thing I would add is: Do not get so caught up in the technical stuff that you fail to *enjoy* your experience. That is, after all, the main idea.

TAPE RECORDERS. To eliminate the hassle of trying to record everything important while making observations, many birders are investing in pocket-size tape recorders. This nifty invention allows you to keep your eyes on your subject while you babble on about all of the terrific things you are seeing. Your hands are free to work your binoculars, and you do not have to worry about dropping your pencil in the pond. Best of all, you can talk faster than you can write, and you will find your notes are really complete when you transcribe them later. The possible complications here are running out of tape, having to turn the tape over during your observation, or discovering the batteries are dead, but these are small potatoes compared to having to interrupt your observation to take notes and realizing the bird went someplace else while you were writing.

Whatever method of note-taking you choose, you should be comfortable with it. If you are not, experiment until you find something that suits you. The best rules to follow here are your own, as long as you obtain quality results.

CHECKLISTS. These are prepared lists of birds that you are likely to see in a given area or range, with a space next to each species for placing a checkmark when you have seen the bird. Since the information that checklists provide is limited to acknowledging the sighting, they are not recommended in place of a field journal; however, they are useful in keeping a count of the species you have seen and for quick overall surveys of particular locations.

LIFE LISTS. These are lists of the species you see in your lifetime. They are similar to the checklist, but they offer a bit more variety since you create these lists from your observations. There are no limits to the variations for a life list, and creative birders can invent a list for nearly everything. Use your imagination and have fun with it. An example is a Year List—the species you see during a given year and variations of that: month, week, day. There are Big Day, Big Week, and Big Month lists. Some birders keep a Backyard List, a Vacation List, and a winter, spring, summer, or fall list. You can keep lists for your favorite birding areas or that you compile driving to and from work, or driving anywhere for that matter. The possibilities are endless.

Listing can become competitive, which in some cases is responsible for that image of the frenzied birder slogging through swamps in pursuit of the elusive quarry. Some birders jet all over the world just to add another species to their lists. In recent years, competitive listing has been employed by Audubon societies and bird clubs as a fund-raising event. Sponsors pledge a certain dollar amount for each species seen, and on the scheduled day, competitive birders follow predetermined routes throughout the state or designated area, each trying to outdo the other.

This type of birding can be great fun, and if maintained over a period of years, lists can provide valuable comparative information. Organized projects making use of listing data (such as the Christmas Bird Count) are discussed in greater detail in Chapter 3.

Shortcuts For Effective Record-Keeping

If you are as enthusiastic about your birding as most naturalists, you will soon begin to accumulate piles of notes on your observations. Since the information you are gathering is only useful if you can find it later, it is important to establish a system for keeping things in order.

One method you may find helpful is the American Ornithologists' Union's (AOU) numerical designation for each species. A complete listing of these numerical classifications is available in the AOU Check-list. (Write the American Ornithologists' Union, c/o National Museum of Natural History, Smithsonian Institution, Washington, D.C. 20560.) If you become involved in banding birds (see chapter 2), you will be required to use the numerical designations in your annual reports.

Though it may sound confusing at first, the AOU numbers prove useful for a variety of reasons. They serve as a cross-reference, are accepted by computer programs, and are understood in many languages. Where the possibility exists that a species' common name may change, the likelihood is that the AOU number will not.

Very briefly, the AOU numbers progress with each species; once you learn the grouping for a particular family it becomes easier to remember the numbers for individuals. Example:

> Sparrow, Vesper   AOU #540
>
> Sparrow, Savannah   AOU #542
>
> Sparrow, Grasshopper   AOU #546

You may also want to learn the standard abbreviations of common birds, developed by Kathleen Klimkiewicz and Chandler Robbins of the Bird Banding Laboratory for the convenience of banders in recording data. The first four letters of a species name become the abbreviation for that species, so that starling is noted as STAR. For a species with two words to a name, such as American robin, the abbreviation is the first two letters of each word: AMRO. Species with more than two words to a name are abbreviated by taking the first letter of the first two words and the first two letters of the last word, so that a white-throated sparrow becomes WTSP.

Although this may sound confusing at first, you will be surprised how easily these abbreviations can be learned and recognized. And once you are accustomed to using the AOU system, you will be lost without it. I use it to file observation records of different species, to organize my research files, and even to keep my collection of slides and photographs in some semblance of order.

Field Techniques for Better Birding

Now that you have all of the necessary equipment, it is time to get out into the field and do something with it! There are many different approaches to field birding. The standard recommendations as to dress and observation techniques are most likely discussed briefly in the front matter of your field guide. Here are a few more helpful hints that I have found effective:

My first suggestion is to act like you belong there, like you are part of the surroundings. Move quietly, but more important, move *naturally*.

Animals are highly sensitive to "body language." Attack dogs, for example, are trained to respond to it—a person walking in a normal manner will be accepted by the dog, but if that same person begins to move stealthily (as someone with malicious intentions will do), the dog will become alert and, depending on the degree of stealth, may very well attack.

My own experiences have led me to believe that if you move stealthily, as a predator would move, you may indeed be able to approach quite closely without being noticed—but more than likely, when you *are* discovered, the wildlife you are watching will retreat as quickly as possible.

Sometimes if you move naturally and with purpose, you can be quite successful in seeing a number of birds and occasionally a few mammals. Predators seldom make much noise when hunting. Therefore, if you move naturally and talk softly, you may find that you are not perceived as an immediate threat. You may even discover that birds especially may come a bit closer to investigate. Admittedly, this technique will not work for everyone, but it has worked on so many occasions for me and several acquaintances that I include it here for your information.

I would also recommend that you try what I call blending. Find yourself a comfortable spot in a promising location, sit or lie on the ground, and do not move. Blend. You will be amazed at the things you will see.

One of my most memorable birding experiences was a result of half an hour's worth of blending. I chose a small clearing in the woods, bordered on one side by a stand of hobblebushes, and on the other by a marsh. It was May 17, a beautiful spring day during the peak of the warbler migration.

After checking my chosen site for spiders (the only thing in nature that slows me down some), I got comfortable, lying on my side with my head propped on my arms. I find that lying on my side enables me to see more without moving, but do whatever is most comfortable for you. I had only been settled in about ten minutes when I was entertained by a black-throated blue warbler in the hobblebushes, about four feet from my head. In the course of a half hour, there were also a wood thrush, an ovenbird, two song sparrows, three goldfinches, and the climax to the show—a common yellowthroat that alighted briefly on the edge of my hiking boot! When we suddenly made eye contact, he squeaked and took off as if shot from a gun. For this kind of birding you need no equipment—just patience and practice. The birds will come to you.

A variation of this technique can be done in winter or fall, by sitting very still and offering sunflower seeds in the palm of your outstretched hand. The key is remaining motionless, as the birds will detect motion before they actually "see" you. If you try this in the woods of New Jersey, I can almost guarantee your first visitor will be a black-capped chickadee—or a chipmunk!

You can also enhance your birding walks by "reading" the

woods, which will provide clues to the species that live there. Inspect the trunks of sugar maple trees for the feeding holes of the yellow-bellied sapsucker. You also will find holes drilled by woodpeckers; sometimes these hold a treasure—an acorn stashed there by the woodpecker as a reserve food supply. Look under ridges in the bark for seeds stashed by nuthatches. Watch also for nesting holes, for droppings under favorite feeding perches, and for the remains of hawk and owl kills. Some of these predators return to the same perches to consume their prey, and the ground under the particular branch will be strewn with feathers and droppings.

Be alert for pellets regurgitated by owls and hawks. The pellets contain bones, fur, teeth and jaws, bird beaks, insect wing cases and "hard parts," feathers, and any other indigestible portions of the raptor's prey.

The pellets of owls are more easily found than those of hawks, since owls especially will use the same roosting and nesting trees and will regurgitate the pellets there. Hawks tend to cast their pellets wherever they happen to be at the moment, and they are usually scattered through the woods.

Owl pellets are quite interesting to study. An owl swallows its prey whole, and their digestive systems, unlike those of diurnal hawks, do not readily digest bone. By studying the pellets of an owl, you can determine the bird's feeding preferences. Sometimes the size and shape of the pellet, combined with the revealed diet and other factors (habitat, location, range, type of roost, and so on) can help you to identify the species.

Pellets do not decay easily, and the ground under a good roosting site may yield a surprising number of them that have accumulated over the years. They are also completely safe to handle (a question that is often asked). The pellets are odorless and do not harbor any harmful substances. Occasionally you will find one that seems to have "worms." These are the larvae of moths, which are harmless to humans, though they will destroy the pellet in time. If you plan to collect pellets, it is a good idea to keep them in mothballs.

When you do find an area strewn with pellets, look up. You may find the owl roosting in the trees, usually near the trunk. Look hard, for they truly have mastered the art of blending.

Another technique for locating birds is to "sweep" an area with your binoculars. Make a slow, deliberate sweep from left to right, watching for movement or color (remember those flash marks). Lower your binoculars a few inches until you have a new level of sight, and scan again in the opposite direction. Continue this sweeping motion until you detect movement. This technique is used exclusively during hawk migrations, where beginning hawkwatchers are astounded at the numbers of birds that suddenly appear in their binoculars, riding on thermals at altitudes beyond the sight of the naked eye.

One of the most productive techniques for field birding, or for any type of outdoor observations, is to be aware of your surroundings as a whole, instead of zeroing in on one specific thing. Even when you are observing an individual, try to keep your other senses alert and tuned in to the whole picture. This takes some practice, but you can do it. Adopt the attitude that, if you do not look at the whole picture, you are going to miss something. After a while, you will be able to see everything.

Reading the woods provides clues to birdlife present. Examples: Owl pellets at base of tree, feather remains on feeding station, evidence of woodpeckers on trees.

Armchair Birding

At first this may seem to be a lazy man's approach to birding, but the truth is that you can enjoy many hours of active birding without ever venturing outdoors.

Chances are the first spark of curiosity that made you become a bird watcher in the first place was generated by watching birds at a feeding station. Perhaps it was the striking contrast of a cardinal in the snow or the sudden appearance of dozens of pine siskins at the window feeder, nose-to-beak with you through the glass.

Observing birds at a feeding station is one of the best places to practice your identification techniques, because feeder birds offer the amateur many advantages. They are easier to locate than field birds. They remain in the same location for extended periods, allowing you ample time to observe, find the bird in your guide, and make notations, and the same species can be observed repeatedly at close range.

Bringing the Birds to You

Establishing a feeding station need not be an expensive or elaborate affair. Certainly you can spend a small fortune on fancy, store-bought feeders, but the *type* of feed you put out, the *location* of the feeding station, and the *consistency* of your feeding program are far more important factors.

Sunflower seed, cracked corn, peanut hearts, white millet, and safflower and thistle seeds are among those most favored by a variety of species. These seeds are available commercially as prepackaged mixes, or you can experiment by purchasing different varieties and creating your own mixes.

There are three major levels of location preference at every feeding station. You can cater to only one if you wish, but if you can accommodate all three, you will attract the greatest variety of species.

For ground-level feeding, the seed is scattered directly across a bare patch of ground. When there is snow, it is preferable to place a piece of plywood or similar material on top of the snow and scatter the seed on it. This will prevent the seed from sinking out of reach. Most sparrows, towhees, juncos, and finches prefer ground-level feeding.

Low-level feeding includes commercially available post-type feeders and low "table-top" feeders. You can use your picnic table or bench for a table-top feeder or build a table for the purpose. You may want to fit the top of your picnic table with a protective covering. Incorporate your natural surroundings whenever possible—an exposed boulder or a sawed-off tree stump can be charming. This is the most popular level of feeding and will attract a variety of species.

Commercially sold hanging feeders or window ledge feeders accommodate the high-level feeding zone. (Hanging feeders are sometimes run out on a clothesline pulley to discourage squirrels, but if you are a true naturalist you will feed the squirrels too.)

Another food source that should be incorporated into every winter feeding program is suet. It can be placed directly on the ground or on table feeders, but it is suggested that you use commercially sold suet feeders or attach the suet as high as you can to the trunk of a tree. The problem with suet placed on ground or table feeders is that it will be stolen by dogs, cats, opossums, and especially raccoons. Don't be too quick to say you don't have any raccoons where you live—you probably just didn't notice—until you put out the suet!

If raccoons are the culprits, there is not much you can do except keep lots of suet on hand. I once watched a very large, winter-fat coon tightrope-walk a six-foot length of clothesline to get at a hanging suet feeder. When the spotlight switch was thrown, catching the bandit in the act and flooding his operation in bright light, he shrugged off this intrusion of his privacy with only a moment's glance in my direction and, holding on with three "hands," shook the line he was straddling with his free hand until the suet feeder fell. He then backed up the length of the line, shimmied down the pole, grabbed his loot, and headed for the woods. I never did find the suet feeder.

There are many fine books dedicated to the subject of feeding wild birds. Consult the recommended reading section of chapter 7.

In addition to establishing a feeding station, planting berry bushes and protective shrubbery and supplying water, nesting sites, and a secure habitat will help attract a large number of birds of different species as well as other wildlife.

The National Wildlife Federation sponsors a program geared to turning your backyard into a wildlife sanctuary. The federation offers a Gardening with Wildlife Kit, which explains how to provide the basic wildlife needs and gives a planting guide; directions for building feeders, birdhouses, and nesting shelves; wildlife fact sheets; and a record-keeping log for your observations.

Your backyard sanctuary may be eligible for certification by the National Wildlife Federation as a NWF Backyard Wildlife Habitat.

Besides the obvious aesthetic qualities of a backyard sanctuary, it will provide you with hours of armchair birding opportunities. What are the food preferences of the birds that visit your feeders? What can you observe about feeding behavior? or flocking behavior? How many birds come in a specified amount of time? What effect does the weather have on feeding habits? How do species interact at the feeders? When do specific migrating species first arrive at the feeders? When do they leave? These are just a few ideas for an interesting project that can be conducted through the window. Feeder studies are a productive and interesting way for handicapped or elderly bird watchers—who find it difficult to get out into the field—to focus their energies.

Feeder Studies

There are quite a few established feeder-related studies underway that welcome contributions by volunteers, and you may want to get your feet wet by participating in one or more of them. The following information will help you get started:

THANKSGIVING BIRD COUNT (TBC). This feeder study originated in 1966—an idea generated by the president of the Lynchburg Bird Club, Mrs. Myriam Moore. Twenty-seven birders participated in the first count, which has been conducted each consecutive year by the Lynchburg Bird Club and Sweet Briar College. Over twenty years later, more than 500 birders from throughout the United States participate in the count.

As the name implies, the count takes place on Thanksgiving Day. Participants count birds that come into an imaginary fifteen-foot horizontal circle around the feeder. The count is continued for one uninterrupted hour. The numbers of individuals for each species observed are recorded on forms provided, and participants also record weather conditions, habitat, types of feeders, and time of observation.

Data collected during the Thanksgiving counts has supported documentation of increases and decreases in overall winter populations, winter dispersal patterns of different species, declines or increases in individual species counts, and expanding or decreasing winter ranges. The data also can be used for a number of comparative studies.

The TBC welcomes all interested persons. Write: Thanksgiving Bird Count, c/o Sweet Briar College, Sweet Briar, VA 24595.

ANNUAL BIRD FEEDER CENSUS. This project is sponsored by the Bird Feeders Society, P.O. Box 243, Mystic, CT 06355. The census is similar to the TBC, but it takes place in February.

MINNESOTA BIRD FEEDER SURVEY. Though this census is designed for Minnesota residents, it offers another variation of the feeder census system of the TBC and the Annual Bird Feeder Census. Observations for the Minnesota census are taken every other weekend, or on two consecutive days in the five weekdays, excluding the weekend. This census requests that participants report only the highest count for a species observed during the observation period.

As you can see from these established projects, the mechanics of conducting a feeder survey are quite simple. You can designate a specified area, such as the fifteen-foot circle, or you can use your entire backyard or as much as you can see

There's no need to slog through a swamp to enjoy birds. Many facets of bird life may be observed and studied through a window.

from your armchair by the window. If you have more than one feeder, why not keep track of which attracts more species and more numbers, and then attempt to determine why.

Choose a day, a weekend, or, if time permits, a larger block of time—a two-week period, a month, the whole winter. The most important factor in any type of research project is consistency. Exactly how you arrive at a consistent method of observation is up to you.

While you are at it, you may want to keep track of what types of foods are taken most often by what species. Much research has been done on this subject, but it still makes a good "practice run" for the beginner, and you will probably have a good time finding things out for yourself.

TWO

HANDS-ON BIRDING

Hands-On Birding

Now that you have mastered the art of armchair birding and are working hard at polishing your field birding techniques, you may want to explore the possibilities of becoming involved in what is a veritable paradise for anyone nurturing an obsession with birds: the bird observatory.

BIRD OBSERVATORIES

Bird observatories are research stations, usually located in areas favorable for observing migrant birds and for studying resident birds. Although they are usually established as large-scale, permanent banding stations, banding is not their only concern. Of the major observatories, most are involved in many different types of natural research, not just ornithology. Many are also involved in public education programs, training workshops and seminars, wildlife rehabilitation, and environmental impact consultation. All things considered, any permanent facility that makes long-term, systematic collections of data could be called an observatory.

The first observatory was organized on a German north sea island, Heligoland, in 1909, but the idea really did not catch on until the end of World War II. There are more than twenty observatories operating in the British Isles. Information on the exact number of observatories in the United States is vague at best. The well-known, major observatories are profiled here, but there may be a few more scattered around the country that have grown (or are in the process of growing) from banding station to observatory.

The importance of bird observatories, like the importance of amateur naturalists, should not be underestimated. Aside from being a mecca for birders and naturalists, observatories bring a sense of permanence and commitment to research that is difficult to match.

The teams of researchers working steadily together on any one project are able to gather more consistent and complete information than anyone working alone possibly could, and the stability of the observatory location affords years of single site baseline data that can be compared to other sites and times.

If you are truly interested in developing your birding interests, I highly recommend you volunteer some time at an observatory. Granted, the scarcity of these facilities may make it difficult, but you will not be sorry. The following is a chronological listing of the major observatories.

Long Point Bird Observatory (Canada)

Long Point Bird Observatory (LPBO), located in Ontario, was the first bird observatory on the North American continent. It was established in 1960 by the Ontario Bird Banding Association, who recognized the need for long-term studies of the Canadian migration. Long Point is a major concentration area for shorebirds, waterfowl, and landbirds during spring and fall, and more than 250,000 birds of 240 species have been banded to date. The observatory encourages cooperation between professional biologists and amateur naturalists, publishing an annual directory of cooperative naturalist's projects in Ontario.

LPBO headquarters are at the Backus Conservation Area, just north of Port Rowan. Banding and migration monitoring takes place at three field stations on Long Point (a twenty-one-mile-long "finger" extending into Lake Erie).

Long Point was instrumental in establishing two additional observatories in Canada: Toronto Bird Observatory (the first city-based facility) and Prince Edward Point Observatory (known for saw-whet owl bandings in the fall). The Hawk Cliff Raptor Banding Station and the Ottawa Banding Group are also closely associated with LPBO.

LPBO welcomes volunteer "assistants"—knowledgeable banders and researchers wishing to volunteer a week or more of their time for migration monitoring at various field stations, some in rather remote areas. Less experienced volunteers also are needed. For information on LPBO and the other Canadian facilities listed above, contact: Long Point Bird

Observatory, P.O. Box 160, Port Rowan, Ontario, Canada
N0E 1M0.

Point Reyes Bird Observatory (California)

Point Reyes Bird Observatory (PRBO) has the distinction of
being the first observatory in America. It was established as a
banding station in 1965, intent on banding and studying
coastal and landbirds in the Point Reyes National Seashore
area.

Today, PRBO conducts research, conservation, and education programs from three year-round locations. The landbird
research and educational programs are headquartered at the
Palomarin Field Station, at the southern entrance to the Point
Reyes National Seashore. Long-term projects here are the
study of landbird migrations and the study of the breeding
ecology of scrub landbird species.

A unique, second location on the Farallon Islands, twenty-
eight miles west of the Golden Gate, is one of the most important seabird and marine mammal breeding areas in the
United States. PRBO biologists and volunteers research and
monitor the wildlife of these islands, and, as a result of
PRBO's protection of the island wildlife, dramatic increases in
many nearly extirpated species have been documented.

PRBO administrative offices and library are located on
Bolinas Lagoon, just north of Stinson Beach in Marin County.
PRBO also offers training programs for volunteer naturalists,
educational interns, and classroom teachers. Contact: Point
Reyes Bird Observatory, 4990 Shoreline Highway, Stinson
Beach, CA 94970.

Manomet Bird Observatory (Massachusetts)

Manomet (MBO) began with a small banding project, called Operation Recovery, whose participants realized the potential, and the need, for a permanent research facility. A gift of an unused summer residence and financial support from several New York and Boston foundations coupled with the hard work and donations from its first members enabled Manomet to begin functioning as a bird observatory. Today, other bird observatories consider MBO a model institution.

Manomet has pioneered the philosophy of gathering baseline data *before* a crisis—not only concerning birds, but the environment as a whole. The nature of MBO's research reflects this. In addition to banding-related studies, MBO has taken on more unusual projects, among them a study of the effects of microwaves on birds.

MBO also welcomes volunteers and trainees. Contact: Manomet Bird Observatory, Box 936, Manomet, MA 02345.

Cape May Bird Observatory (New Jersey)

Cape May Bird Observatory (CMBO) was established in 1975 by the New Jersey Audubon Society, primarily as a site to monitor the migration of hawks through Cape May Point in the fall. However, like its colleagues, CMBO has expanded into many areas of natural history research.

Cape May is staffed by two full-time biologists, working with volunteers and interns. CMBO is currently studying shorebird concentrations in the Delaware Bay and monitoring the population and ecology of harriers in the coastal wetlands. It also conducts an annual bald eagle survey and numerous small mammal studies, and it supports the research projects initiated by the New Jersey Audubon Society.

CMBO accepts participation from volunteers with a strong background in field ornithology or biology, especially those with banding or field trip experience.

Contact: Cape May Bird Observatory, P.O. Box 3, 707 East Lake Drive, Cape May Point, NJ 08212.

San Francisco Bay Bird Observatory (California)

San Francisco Bay Bird Observatory (SFBBO) is one of the nation's newest, organized in 1982. Like its colleagues, SFBBO was established as a banding and field research station. It currently operates one of the country's few (possibly the only) riparian banding stations at Coyote Creek.

Projects at SFBBO include studying the California clapper rail, monitoring the breeding colonies of the California gull, and studying raptor and hummingbird biology and salt marsh common yellowthroats.

SFBBO has an active rehabilitation program and is currently investigating the cause, effects, and treatment of avian botulism.

If you wish to participate as a volunteer, contact: San Francisco Bay Bird Observatory, 1290 Hope Street, P.O. Box 247, Alviso, CA 95002.

Raccoon Ridge Bird Observatory (New Jersey)

My own involvement with birds, which is what happens to you when you are no longer content with watching, really began at the Raccoon Ridge Bird Observatory. It was there that I learned to band birds and to channel my interest and enthusiasm into worthwhile projects.

Raccoon Ridge (RRBO) was an independent, nonprofit organization formed in 1975—the first in New Jersey—by its director, Dorothy Hughes, and a handful of volunteers. It was unique in that it kept pace with the other observatories—amassing rooms of research material, establishing itself as a strong research center in northern New Jersey, organizing and conducting the New Jersey atlas project—all without a paid staff.

RRBO was initially established within the Delaware Water Gap National Recreation Area and later moved to the grounds of the Linwood MacDonald Environmental Education Center near Stokes State Forest. RRBO also established satellite banding stations in several other locations in northern New Jersey.

In addition to the atlas project, RRBO conducted banding-related studies, monitored the migration of raptors and other birds along the Kittatinny mountain range, conducted environmental studies within the park area, sponsored a training program for banders and volunteers, and maintained wildlife rehabilitation and public education programs.

Although Raccoon Ridge Bird Observatory has ceased operations as a banding station, research information is available by contacting director Dorothy Hughes, 1302 63rd Street West, Bradenton, FL 33510.

In 1977, when I visited Raccoon Ridge for the first time, it was located within the Delaware Water Gap National Recreation Area. I had no idea it was there, only a forty-five minute drive from my home, until I happened across a "Letter to the Editor" in the local paper, written by an elementary school teacher. The teacher thanked RRBO for presenting a banding program and demonstration to her students, and she recommended that area residents visit the facility.

That schoolteacher will never know what she did for me. I called RRBO the same day, explaining to John who answered the phone that I would like to write an article about RRBO and could I make an appointment to visit them soon? John, with a hint of State o' Maine in his speech and a welcoming tone of voice, told me to "come on up in the morning around six" because his wife Dot and a few volunteers would be there banding.

I went there with all the professional intentions of writing a good feature article. Instead, I became so involved in the experience that the article was pushed to the back of my mind. Dot was on the porch of the historic stone mansion that the National Park Service had provided as a headquarters for the observatory, an ovenbird gently cradled in the palm of her hand.

In spite of years of birding, the only *really* close-up birds I had seen were dead ones. This was altogether different. Dot instructed me on the proper way to hold the bird, guiding my fingers to the right places as she positioned the ovenbird in my hand.

Any thoughts of writing were forgotten as I felt the vibrations of the creature in my hand. I marveled on how relaxed the bird seemed, on the form and color of each feather, of the whiteness of the breast in contrast with the brown spots that decorated it, of the secrets of flying and migration and navigation and nesting and living all packaged neatly in that tiny head, gift wrapped in feathers. The bird and I exchanged looks, and I knew I was on the brink of a whole new way of life.

Dot explained the process as she placed the band around the bird's leg, took measurements of the wing length, checked the plumage for parasites, weighed the bird, and (all in the space of about three minutes) set it free. It flew to the hedgerow at the end of the lawn, paused on a twig to rouse its ruffled feathers and dignity, and disappeared into the brush. Dot turned to me and offered to teach me to band.

BANDING

The earliest record of banding (or as it is known in Europe, "ringing") a bird for the purpose of identifying an individual dates back to Asia, circa 1275 to 1295, and Marco Polo's observations of "marked" captive falcons. During the Roman Empire, birds were marked for other purposes. Parent swallows were taken from their nests in Volterra to the chariot races in Rome. Threads bearing the race winner's colors were attached to each swallow's legs. The birds—being anxious to return to their young—flew hastily back to Volterra, carrying the results of the Roman races to Volterra's residents.

There are scattered accounts of marking experiments throughout history. One report tells of a heron marked with a twist of wire in Turkey in 1710 and recovered later in Germany. During the late 1890s, Hans Christian Mortensen, a schoolteacher in Viborg, Denmark, began placing metal bands on the legs of ducks, teals, storks, starlings, and hawks. No one paid much attention, until the "banded" birds began appearing in different countries across Europe.

John James Audubon is credited with being the first American bander. Audubon's curiosity about a family of phoebes nesting under a stone bridge prompted him to mark the birds, hoping this would help him to determine if the birds he observed each year were the same individuals. They were.

In 1909 the American Bird Banding Association was organized. Eventually wildlife biologists in the Bureau of Biological Survey (now the U.S. Fish and Wildlife Service) and the Canadian Wildlife Service recognized the importance of banding, and in 1920 the American Bird Banding Association relinquished the responsibility of organizing banders to them. Since that time, all banding of migratory birds has been directed jointly by the U.S. and Canadian governments.

Today, banding is a sophisticated, well-regulated activity. The Bird Banding Laboratory (BBL) of the Fish and Wildlife Service, located in the Patuxent Wildlife Research Center in Laurel, Maryland, issues every band used in the United States, Canada, Latin America, and Mexico. The BBL computers keep track of thousands of bands that are recovered each year—a small percentage compared to the million or more birds that are marked annually, but valuable information nevertheless.

Bands are presized to fit every size bird. They are stamped with an identifying number, which is never duplicated on another band (sort of like a social security number for birds). The band is also stamped, "AVISE BIRD BAND/WRITE WASH DC USA." The word "avise" is used because in Spanish, French, Portuguese, and Latin-based languages it means "report" or "tell." It is close enough to the English "advise" for most people to figure out. So what do you do when you find a banded bird?

If the bird is dead, you can remove the band. It is a butt-end ring that will come apart easily with needle-nose pliers. Removing the band should be attempted only if the bird is dead. Obviously, removing the band from a live bird defeats the purpose, and you also run the risk of breaking the bird's leg.

Flatten the removed band, and tape it to a piece of paper with your name, address, where you found the bird, how it was killed (if you know that), and the date and time. Mail the band to the Bird Banding Laboratory, U.S. Fish and Wildlife Service, Laurel, MD 20708. Every so often, someone will mail the whole bird to the Banding Lab. That's really not necessary—the band will do nicely. If you think, however, that the Banding Lab might be interested in receiving the whole bird (unusual circumstances, uncommon species, and so on), contact them for permission.

Sometimes, birds fly into a house and must be released, or they are temporarily stunned when they hit a window. In this case, write the band numbers on a piece of paper with the information listed above, and send it to the BBL.

You will receive, eventually, a certificate of appreciation from the BBL, telling you what kind of bird you found, where and when and by whom it was banded, and its age and sex if known.

Though the ratio may be low, almost seventy years' worth of banding recoveries have revealed avian secrets we otherwise would not have known. Beside the obvious advantages of being able to study the bird in the hand, banding has given us the means of identifying an individual, and with that the ability to monitor the movements, migration routes, lifespans, and a host of related life history information.

When birds are banded, released, and recaptured by other banders, we can piece together their migration flyways. We know that a pintail duck banded in Louisiana flew to China. We know that a black duck banded on Cape Cod was shot in Newfoundland seventeen years later, and that a herring gull banded on the nest in Maine in 1930 was discovered dead on a Lake Michigan shoreline in 1966. We know the Arctic tern makes a migratory flight of some 25,000 miles from recoveries in North America, South Africa, France, Nigeria, and Cape Province.

Banding recoveries also give us information on how far and how fast some birds are capable of traveling. Two blue-winged teals, banded at Long Point, were recovered in Brazil. LPBO received recovery information from Mexico on a sharp-shinned hawk, from Guatemala for a cedar waxwing, from Jamaica for a Cape May warbler, and from Colombia for a rose-breasted grosbeak. A report of a Swainson's thrush banded at Long Point and recovered the next day at Prince Edward Point proved the bird flew some 310 kilometers overnight.

Birds that are banded in one location and recaptured in the same location at a later date are called "returns." From these records we can monitor stops along the migration routes and estimate arrival and departure times. Returns also supply information on breeding and habitat preferences. In one season, my own backyard banding station was graced with these returns:

A black-and-white warbler banded on 5/30/79 returned

on 5/14/80; a veery banded on 5/22/80 returned on 5/6/81; a yellowthroat banded on 5/15/80 returned on 5/8/81; a catbird banded on 7/12/80 returned on 5/9/81; and another catbird banded on 5/4/80 returned on 5/14/81.

Believe me, this kind of experience can add tremendous excitement to your birding habit. During later years at the RRBO, I was asked by a visitor why we banded birds. The first response that shot out of my mouth was "because it's fun." Dot nearly fell off her chair—being the proper research biologist—and I suppose I should have first explained the important, scientific reasons for what we were doing. But banding *is* fun, and I do enjoy it, and enjoying your birding habit while contributing to the science of ornithology is what this book is all about. Banding adds a whole new dimension to the birding experience. It certainly stimulates my curiosity. Now when I am out birding during spring migration, instead of saying "Oh, look, it's a black-and-white warbler" and noting it in my journal, I am full of questions. Is it the same one? Is he banded? Where has he been all winter? How did he get there? If it is the same one, how did he find his way back here, to this same patch of woods? How old is he now? Will he nest here? How has he changed since we met last? Does he weigh the same? Measure the same? Is it a he or a she? Can that be determined yet? Let's see: It's not banded. It's a different bird.

A bird in the hand will teach you to be more observant and to pay more attention to detail than any bird in the field. The first bird I ever banded is a perfect example. It was fall, and the bird Dot handed me was one of those nondescript olive-drab fall warblers. I was pretty good at identifying warblers in the field, but this bird and I looked at each other, and he never gave me a clue. There was no movement here, no habitat to consider, no elevation, character quirks or distinctive habits, no song, no chirps, no calls, no interaction with other warblers. Nothing. Only a passive olive-green bird vibrating softly in my hand. This was a whole new ballgame.

Well, for starters, I knew it was a warbler. Going through the banding manual and array of field guides on the table pointed out about twenty or so possibilities. Egads. I began to look for finer details. No wing bars. No tail spots. That narrowed the field to about eleven. Better, but not much. I could not decide if the bird had an eye ring. It certainly was not very distinct, yet if I held the bird at arm's length it looked like there could be the faintest little ring right there.

I decided to go with the eye ring. When I had finally narrowed my choices to two prime-looking suspects on the pages of the banding manual, Dot peered over my shoulder. With the sharpened point of a pencil, she gently raised the feathers on the bird's head. A single, rust-colored feather appeared out of nowhere. Of course. How obvious. Nashville warbler, sex unknown, fall plumage.

In the weeks that followed, I found myself migrating to RRBO every morning, arriving at the Old Mine Road Youth Hostel Banding Station around six-thirty to help open nets and prepare for the morning's birds.

The youth hostel station, located within the Delaware Water Gap National Recreation Area, a few hundred yards from the Delaware River, was a phenomenal banding site. We found that birds followed the river during migrations, resting and feeding around the hostel during the day. Birds were everywhere! A month before I began working at RRBO, a varied thrush (a western species) made its appearance in the apple orchard on the front lawn. Birders from New Jersey and neighboring states congregated at the hostel to see this rare visitor. Dot and the crew served gallons of coffee and repeatedly bought out the local bakery during the varied thrush's short stay at the hostel, but attempts at netting and banding the bird were unsuccessful. Its appearance, however, helped to put the fledgling RRBO on the map.

In 1978, RRBO succeeded in netting another rare visitor, a northern shrike. Though not as unusual in the area as the varied thrush, the bird is still considered a rare sighting in northwestern New Jersey. More commonly, this bird breeds in northern Quebec, occasionally wintering south into Pennsylvania. It is a difficult bird to see in the field, since it will retreat rapidly when approached. To have one in the net was an experience to remember—especially for Dot, who was unanimously elected by her banding trainees to remove the bird from the net.

She did so somewhat gingerly, since the shrike was quite capable of drawing blood and was anything but passive in the hand. "That is the nastiest, meanest, most ill-tempered critter," Dot said later, nursing more than one cut and bruised finger to prove it.

The northern shrike is known also as a "butcher bird," from the practice of impaling its prey—small birds, rodents, frogs, reptiles, and large insects—on thorns. This practice probably evolved to compensate for the shrike's lack of taloned feet, which are not designed for grasping and holding prey, as are the taloned feet of hawks and owls. Instead of using its feet to hold and kill, the shrike's formidable beak is its weapon. The bird overtakes its prey and uses its beak to kill.

A few years later, in 1981, RRBO interns discovered another rare visitor, a Townsend's solitaire, on Sunrise Mountain during a hawkwatch. RRBO reported the bird to New Jersey Audubon's "Rare Bird Alert," and again prominent ornithologists and amateur birders from New Jersey and neighboring states responded by flocking to the mountain.

Birds are captured in mist nets or traps, depending on the season. Mist nets are constructed of fine mesh, usually nylon, similar to old-fashioned hairnets. They are available in various sizes, the most common being about forty feet long and six feet high. The net is in four loosely constructed tiers, called trammels. Nets are usually strung in natural "lanes" along shrubbery, or in lanes cleared for the purpose. An open net is surprisingly hard to detect (I have caught a few people along the way). Birds do not see it either, unless there is a breeze blowing, or there is a leaf or something in the net to give it away. I have watched many birds head straight for it, only to fly up and over at the last minute. If you are lucky and they do not detect the net, they will fly into it, bounce into the trammels, and become tangled, where they must await rescue by the bander. Removing a bird from the net is not as difficult as it first appears to be, but it does require special training and a certain amount of manual dexterity. Banders wishing to use mist nets must receive specialized training to do so, and their banding permits will specify the number of nets they are licensed to operate.

Nets are never left unattended; it is wise to check them every fifteen minutes. When not in use, they are either taken down completely, or "closed"—furled and tied. When it rains, nets are closed. Wet birds should not be handled; they tend to lose feathers and are easily chilled. Handling also removes some of the protective oil from their feathers, which is needed in a storm to repel water. The nets are closed, or checked more frequently, if they are in hot sunshine, and when the wind is strong enough to hinder getting birds out quickly. Nets are also closed when the bander is catching more birds than he or she can comfortably process in a short period of time.

There are many types of traps employed for banding purposes. Most are designed to capture birds at a feeding station, but there are also traps for cavity-nesting birds and for raptors. Probably the most commonly used design is called the potter's trap, which is used to trap birds at a feeding station. Birds enter the cagelike trap and are harmlessly held until they are removed by the bander.

The process of netting and banding birds sometimes offends avid bird watchers, who question the need for inflicting so much stress on a wild bird. Some birders downright dislike banders, until they are invited to participate. It has been my experience that the few skeptics I have encountered seem to change their attitudes once they understand that the birds are not harmed, and that the whole process usually takes less than five minutes. When they are given the opportunity to see, up close, what they have been trying to focus in their binoculars for years, and when the bird is released moments later with nothing more serious than a few ruffled feathers, the skeptics usually ask how I got involved in this and could they hang around and watch some more and maybe even help out somehow?

During one particular banding demonstration, while I

was attempting to reassure a rather stuffy bird club member that the birds were not molested, I was unexpectedly assisted by "Ole Number 96." This was a "repeat" black-capped chickadee referred to as "96" from the last two digits of his band number. I should explain here that a "repeat" is just what it says—a bird caught more than once in the same location during a very short time frame. Number 96 was a chronic repeat.

As our little troop approached the net, I knew 96 was going to help me out with this one. He was as fiesty as ever, and as I worked at freeing the little devil, he scolded and screamed, hammering away at my fingers as I tried to unravel the rats-nest of mesh he had gripped in his toes. He seemed to take some sort of pleasure in creating this black mass of twisted threads in my net. I could almost hear the tongue-clicking in the group of birders gathered around me. I started talking as I manipulated the black thread from around the chickadee's toes.

"We'll just take this bird in and weigh him. He has been caught in this net forty-five times this season, twice this week and it's only Tuesday. I have a pretty accurate record of his weight gain and loss, which in turn tells me something about his feeding habits. He was first banded here eighteen months ago as a hatching year bird. He's lived here in these woods ever since. He's a regular at the feeders in the winter and is in the traps at least once a day, sometimes more. He knows how they work, and can hop in, take his seeds, and hop out without getting caught, but sometimes he is, because another bird gets caught and bumps the door shut behind him. When that happens, he eats all the sunflower seed he can manage before I let him out. I've watched him put on fat for winter nights, and lose it by morning. I've watched him moult; once I treated him for feather mites, and he raised a brood of four young in that dead tree by the house. Let me introduce you."

By the time that banding demonstration was over, the stuffy birders had loosened up and were asking if they could come back during fall migration. They did (and so did 96).

I should mention that you should not think of assisting at a bird observatory with hopes of receiving a paycheck for your services. Most limit their paid staff members to two or three biologists, relying on volunteers, interns, temporary grants, and private sector funding for financial support. If you can manage it, do not let the lack of funds stop you from getting involved. I worked at RRBO for eight years as a volunteer. The learning experiences and "hands-on" opportunities I had will be with me forever, and I draw from them everyday.

The rewards of working with nature cannot be measured monetarily. How can you put a price on having the opportunity to spend a fine spring morning outdoors, deeply involved with wildlife and nature? The anticipation of what treasure you will find in your nets alone makes it worthwhile. I will never forget my first hummingbird—so tiny, so perfect. Or my first hawk. So powerful, so wild. You cannot put a dollar value on holding a hummingbird or a hawk in your hand.

Then there were the children—hundreds of them who came to RRBO for banding demonstrations. They sat in a circle on the front lawn, while the blue jays and sparrows made the rounds. Tough little boys and squealing girls—some too bold and some scared half to death—each of whom mustered enough courage to allow one, tentative finger to touch a feathered back. In that instant, in that smile and giggle, you knew that this wild creature had made a lasting impression, opened up new horizons, put things into a different perspective.

There were other priceless moments. Releasing the recovered red-tailed hawk in the field, watching her fly strong and free after months of care and therapy; running for the canoe and a fishing net to rescue the just-released herring gull, which apparently did not have enough oil on its feathers and was quietly sinking lower and lower into the lake; having two busloads of campers arrive for a banding demonstration, and not catching any birds; having a hysterical woman bang on the door, an injured bird in the shoebox, begging for help (the bird was already dead, but I explained gently, "It's in shock, we'll just let it rest here awhile." I gave her a cup of tea and assured her I would do everything I could to save the bird, and she said she would stay until it recovered from the shock); a whole family coming to watch the release of the orphan they rescued; walking out the door and being surrounded by seven released fledglings that still wanted me to feed them; and a little girl on the front porch, clutching a sick pet chicken, and that same little girl thanking me through happy tears when the chicken could go home again.

ALTERNATIVES TO BIRD OBSERVATORIES

An alternative to a bird observatory, and probably easier to find, would be a nature center or local Audubon Society chapter. Most communities have such a facility within reach, and many accept volunteer participation. There may or may not be a bander in residence, but most facilities are involved in some type of wildlife research or educational programs.

Your state Fish and Wildlife office, county park commission, and local library are all sources of information for locating and contacting facilities in your area.

If observatories are so great (you may be thinking), why aren't there more of them? It may be because of the vast number of small, individual banding stations scattered across the country. These are the "personal" observatories of thousands of amateur naturalists and banders. More than a million birds are banded each year in the United States by federally licensed, volunteer amateur ornithologists, people like me and you.

Requirements for obtaining a banding license are that you be at least eighteen years of age, that you can reasonably identify the common birds of North America in different plumages, and that you have a reason for wanting to band. "Because it's fun" is not acceptable! Banding is a tool for research, and therefore you must have a research project. You may wish to study the species that breed and migrate through a given area; you may wish to study the breeding biology of a particular species, or many species; or you may wish to monitor migration. Banding lends support and "proof" to almost any project, and justifying your desire for a banding permit should pose no problems for you. An additional requirement is that you are endorsed by three licensed banders or known ornithologists. This is not as complicated as it sounds, especially if you are fortunate enough to live near a licensed bander. The BBL can furnish you with the names and addresses of banders near you. Most are more than willing to take on a banding student. When your instructor feels you are capable

Migration routes of many species have been plotted as a result of banding returns.

of banding on your own, he or she may obtain a "subpermit" for you. This will allow you to band without your instructor being present, and it will give you a chance to see if you are interested enough to apply for your own master permit.

An alternative to having no suitable research facility near you is to start your own. This, of course, will depend on many factors. Though it is not necessary to be an ornithological expert, a good basic knowledge of birds certainly will help. You should be thoroughly familiar with migrating and resident species in your area, and a few years of banding experience will be to your benefit. You will need to formulate a working plan and be able to handle the "business" aspect of this type of facility. There will be visitors, requests for information from other facilities, calls for rehabilitation help, and so on. You will need a way to maintain financial backing, and you must keep meticulous records for tax purposes (most research facilities are nonprofit organizations).

Of course, you do not have to do this alone. With a professional approach and clearly defined goals, you should be able to locate banders, researchers, and volunteers to help you.

There is another alternative to the type of organization mentioned above—the private, "backyard" research station. The amateur naturalist with an average working knowledge of birds can, without too much difficulty, establish a productive and important private facility that will bring (if nothing else) years of personal satisfaction.

You may not call it a "bird observatory" in the beginning—maybe it will be a "field station" or simply a "banding station"—but keep in mind that more than one of the full-fledged bird observatories in operation today began as backyard stations.

The following suggestions are intended as a starting point for your ideas—a sampling of things you may want to take into consideration.

Assuming you are the owner of a nice parcel of land, located slightly off the beaten track, with a few outbuildings, electricity, and running water available; and assuming that your land is located within a flyway or, by virtue of its bird-attracting habitats and food supply, hosts a variety of migrant and resident birds; and assuming that you have no other long-range plans for this parcel of paradise, you are in business.

If, on the other hand, you live in an apartment and store all your birding gear in the trunk of your car, it is obvious you will have to follow another route. Your best sources for a possible site are within state and county parks, wildlife refuges, and Audubon sanctuaries. A banding station or field research station that will not be open to the public can be operated on private land after, of course, obtaining written permission from the owner.

Try to pick a site that offers a variety of habitats, including a source of water. If water is not available, you can provide it alongside your feeding stations.

Other sources of banding sites are scouting and private camps, especially if you volunteer to present a series of banding programs to the scouts or campers. This can prove to be a rewarding experience all around, since scouts often get involved in your programs by building birdhouses and helping to maintain banding lanes.

I should warn you here and now that this tends to snow-ball. One day you will be happily operating a small, private banding station, and before you know it you will be involved in half a dozen different studies and laying plans in your head for half a dozen more. It is the nature of the work.

If you are considering a bird observatory somewhere down the line, you will need to formulate an overall plan of what you hope to accomplish. Actually, this is not a bad idea for a small private station to do, either. What activities you become involved with will depend somewhat on your location. Obviously you will not be monitoring the breeding habits of seabirds if your station is located in the middle of Kansas. No matter where you are located, though, you will find work to be done in the areas of habitat usage and preservation, breeding behavior and ecology, threatened and endangered species, migrating species, resident populations and behavior, and life-history studies of individual species. You may also find your-self studying the local mammals, plants, insects, amphibians, fish, reptiles, and anything else that walks, flies, or swims through your area.

One area that should not be overlooked is teaching what you have learned, and are learning, to others. Elementary schools are constantly searching for quality programs for their students, as are scouting organizations, civic groups, adult garden and birding clubs, senior citizen groups . . . the list goes on.

A field trip to your station, where you explain what you are doing and why, can be beneficial to you as well as your vis-itors. Many will make a contribution towards your efforts. Others will help with donations of birdseed, banding supplies, birdhouses and feeders, and other equipment. Appreciation and enthusiasm for your program will spread, and you will be contacted by other groups seeking similar programs. You may want to develop a slide program about your work to present to people who cannot come to you. You may acquire a few volunteers to help with your research and daily operations. You will gain a reputation for "knowing," and may soon find yourself applying for "salvaged wildlife" permits from federal and state governments to allow you to care for birds and animals people will bring to you. You will no doubt begin building flight cages and gathering supplies for raising orphaned young. As your reputation builds, you may find various community and environmental groups contacting you for environmental consultation. As your data accumulate, you will begin to analyze your findings, and possibly publish them in professional journals. I warned you that this has a tendency to snowball.

Again, these ideas are meant to jog your imagination a little bit, to illustrate the potential that you, the amateur naturalist, can become more than a "watcher." If it sounds a little overwhelming, don't let it frighten you. When you are ready, you will slide right into it before you even know what is happening.

THREE

COOPERATIVE BIRDING—
ATLASES, SURVEYS, COUNTS

Cooperative Birding—
Atlases, Surveys, Counts

There are numerous cooperative research projects that offer excellent opportunities for amateur naturalists. Through these projects you will be gaining practical birding knowledge, getting plenty of practice in collecting data, having fun, and contributing to major ornithological projects of lasting value.

BREEDING BIRD ATLASES

As the name implies, the objective of an atlas is to map the distribution of breeding birds in any given area. What makes this breeding survey different from others is that the "given area" is an entire state, an entire country, and eventually an entire continent. It is also unique in another respect. While many projects welcome participation by amateurs, the atlas absolutely depends on it—and it is by far the most accurate, certainly the most ambitious, and probably one of the most important birding surveys ever developed. It is also a new idea, ornithologically speaking, but in less than twenty years, atlasers are literally covering the globe in worldwide efforts. Not bad for a bunch of amateurs!

The atlas seed germinated in Great Britain, during the mid 1960s. An influential group of British ornithologists had before them the *Atlas of the British Flora*, a 1962 publication that culminated the efforts of 1,500 botanists, working together to map the distribution of about 2,000 plant species in Great Britain. The botanists had divided the country into ten-kilometer squares and surveyed the plants found within each square. It had taken them ten years to do this.

The ornithologists speculated that what would work with plants should also work for birds, but a few modifications would be necessary. Ten years would be too long, as habitats and ranges changed too quickly. How would you know you have accounted for all species—a bird does not sit still like a plant. When you did find a bird, how would you prove it was breeding? And above all, was it worth it?

After much consultation and planning, members of the British Trust for Ornithology and the Irish Wildbird Conservancy agreed on specific modifications, and the first Breeding Bird Atlas was launched. It would cover the entire British Isles, and it would be completed in five years' time. Birds would be placed in one of three breeding categories—possible breeders, probable breeders, and confirmed breeders—depending on behavioral observations matched against a code of breeding evidence criteria.

The British atlasers, 12,000 of them, covered 4,000 ten-kilometer squares within the five-year period, filling out

95,000 reporting cards for 218 breeding species. The result, *The Atlas of Breeding Birds in Britain and Ireland*, published in 1976, became the blueprint for other countries to follow.

And follow they did. Even while British atlasers were collecting breeding records for their project, ornithologists around the globe were organizing atlases of their own. In 1971, the European Ornithological Atlas Committee was formed to coordinate all European projects, so that they would be uniform in the methods they used. Over a period of time, atlases were conducted and published in Denmark, France, West Germany, Berlin, Bavaria, Netherlands, Spain, Natal, Australia, Tasmania, New Zealand, Hungary, Switzerland, Czechoslovakia, and Finland. Other countries, among them Uganda, Zaire, Kenya, Zimbabwe, Somalia, Turkey, Poland, and Sweden, are in various stages of planning and field work.

The atlas found its way to the United States via Chan Robbins through the Maryland Ornithological Society. Birders in Montgomery County organized a pilot project, patterned after the British atlas but surveying sixty ten-square-mile blocks over a period of three years. The ten-mile blocks were created by dividing the U.S. Geological Survey (7.5-minute scale) topographic maps for the state of Maryland into six equal portions. The resulting blocks measured roughly ten square miles.

Massachusetts was the first to take on a statewide atlas, followed shortly by Vermont, Maine, New York, New Hampshire, and New Jersey. By 1988, several East Coast states had completed their field work; the Vermont, Maine, Ontario, and New York atlases were published; and more than a dozen were underway or in the planning stages all across the country. Atlases are easier to find than bird observatories.

Getting involved in an atlas project will give you some practical field experience in behavior observation techniques, collecting and recording data, working alone or with other birders, and a real sense of accomplishment. It also will get you out into the field more often, during seasons you otherwise might let slip by. What you will learn from atlasing can be applied to other projects.

The atlas idea may sound a bit overwhelming at first, but the mechanics of the project are really quite simple. As a volunteer, you will be assigned the block of your choice (if you have no preference and are willing to travel, you may be assigned a block that no one else has surveyed). There may be other atlasers in your block, and you may want to contact them to compare notes. You need not worry about duplicating information, since you are looking only for the presence and breeding status of a species within your block. If another atlaser submits the same records, there is no harm done. In fact, it may prove beneficial—you may have observed a higher degree of breeding evidence than your colleague, and therefore the species could be upgraded. (Upgrading is explained below.) Duplications will become apparent when the data are analyzed. Of course, you can choose to atlas more than one block, as long as you keep your observation records straight. On the other hand, if the thought of covering a ten-square-mile-block is scaring you off, not to worry. You do not have to do the whole block if you really cannot. The coordinator of the project will see to it that the block is adequately covered before the field work is finished.

One effective way to ensure that a block will be adequately covered also originated in Britain, though the British, being ever-so-proper, called it "square-a-day surveying." Americans thought the term was boring and opted to use "block busting" or "square-creaming" instead. At any rate, you get the picture.

The idea is to organize the troops and systematically survey the whole block in one shot. This technique is especially valuable in remote areas, and probably every atlas project in existence has had to resort to this method at one time or another.

Remember that whatever you contribute is important, even if it is only one record. Think of the atlas as a jigsaw puzzle. Just one missing piece ruins the whole picture.

When you volunteer as an atlaser, you will receive a "data card" or similar field record card, which you will return to your area coordinator or the main atlas office at the end of the breeding season. The data card will be a checklist of birds suspected of breeding in your state, with columns for possible, probable, and confirmed breeding. You also will receive full instructions, but we will take a closer look at atlasing here so you will have an idea of what is involved.

You should receive a photocopied map of your block with your instructions kit. If you do not, you can purchase the topographical maps in sporting goods stores or by writing directly to the U.S. Geological Survey (907 National Center, 12201 Sunrise Valley Drive, Reston, VA 22092).

When your kit arrives, you should sit down with your map and become familiar with its boundaries. Observations made outside of them belong in a different block. Familiarize yourself with roads, where you can get to specific areas by car, and where you will have to walk. Secure the names of property owners from the tax map at your municipal building, and contact them for permission to survey their property. Most landowners are more than willing to participate. This little bit of extra work on your part will ensure a smoother time in the field, and you need to do it only once.

You should also spend some time in the field getting acquainted with and identifying the different habitats. You may want to create your own list of "expected" birds according to habitat, and be sure to look for these species when you actually begin atlasing. You should also familiarize yourself with the criteria code for breeding evidence. This code, standardized for use in all American atlases, will tell you what you should be looking for in the field, and determines how you will report an observation.

CRITERIA FOR POSSIBLE BREEDING. This is the lowest category of breeding evidence. It is indicated with an "X" marked in the appropriate column of your data card. The code states that a species observed during the breeding season in a possible nesting habitat, or a singing male observed during breeding season, are all the criteria you need to list the bird as a possible breeder. After that point, the code becomes more specific.

CRITERIA FOR PROBABLE BREEDING. This is a single letter code, entered in the appropriate column. The criteria for probable birds becomes more demanding:

P   for Pair observed in a suitable habitat duing breeding season.

S   for Singing male, heard or observed on more than one occasion in the same place.

Locating a nest is only one means of confirming a breeding; alternate criteria include adults carrying food and recently fledged young.

T   for a bird or pair who hold Territory (chasing other individuals).

D   for Courtship or Display, or agitated behavior or anxiety calls of adults, and copulation. For banders, this includes a well-developed brood patch or cloacal protuberance on trapped adults.

N   for birds observed visiting a probable Nest site.

S   for nest building by wrens and woodpeckers. Since wrens often build more than one nest and woodpeckers excavate roosting cavities, these observations cannot be considered proof of breeding evidence for these species.

CRITERIA FOR CONFIRMED BREEDING. This is the highest category, and logging a bird as confirmed is the goal of the atlaser. A double-letter code is entered in the appropriate column:

DD   for Distraction Display or injury feigning. The broken wing routine of the killdeer, and the injury display of the ruffed grouse are examples.

NB   for Nest Building by any species except wrens and woodpeckers, as noted above.

UN   for Used Nest found. This code must be used with caution; you must be sure to identify the nest correctly.

FE   for Female with egg in oviduct. Primarily for banders but also used for road and window-killed birds.

FL   for *recently* Fledged young. Use this with caution because fledglings of certain species will travel great distances shortly after fledging, and they may have hatched in a different block. This is most effective for birds that are obvious recent fledglings, still being fed by their parents.

FS   for adult carrying Fecal Sac.

FY   for adult with Food for Young. This is also used with caution: some species (gulls, terns, raptors) continue to feed their young long after they have fledged, by which time they may have moved a considerable distance. Also some species carry food considerable distances (terns); be careful near edges of blocks.

ON   for adult(s) entering or leaving a nest site in circumstances indicating an Occupied Nest. This is not generally used for open nesting birds, but for hole nesters when a bird enters an appropriate hole and remains inside or leaves a hole after having been inside for some time.

NE   for Nest with Eggs. Also for a bird incubating eggs, or eggshells found below a nest.

NY   Nest with Young.

As you can see by studying the criteria code, as an atlaser, you will be paying much closer attention to what the birds are doing than if you were just out to add to your life list.

To some people, the atlas sounds like a massive invasion of avian privacy, harboring risks of widespread nest-desertions by species that, during critical breeding periods, cannot tolerate such close encounters with humans.

Atlasers, of course, tend to disagree. When you read that the "goal is to confirm as many species as possible within the block," your initial thought is you have to find the actual nest. But, if you look at the criteria code, there are many alternative behavioral choices, many that can be accomplished from a fair distance.

Atlasers, because of the very nature of what they are trying to accomplish, are generally respectful of the bird and its place in the environment. Most are very careful about needlessly approaching a nest and refrain from prolonged observation. It is probably safe to say that an atlaser will cause less of a hazard than a competitive lister bent on adding another lifer to his list.

Precautions have also been taken to protect the nesting locations of threatened and endangered species. The British organizers devised a system whereby the "secret" records of endangered species were seen by no one except the national organizer. When the maps for each endangered species were published, the symbols indicating breeding records were misplaced on the map and so noted. Some American atlases have opted to eliminate showing individual blocks in the state, and instead are simply saying whether or not the bird was located. The system seems to produce maps that are as accurate as possible under the circumstances, without publicizing critical nesting locations of endangered species.

Another point that should be noted is that an atlas is not a census. As an atlaser, you are not asked to count the birds you see. You are only interested in the *species*, and once a species is confirmed within your block, you have fulfilled your responsibility.

Okay, you have checked your topographical map, staked out your territory, brushed up on your identification techniques, dusted off the field guides, and cleaned your binoculars. Where do you start?

At about five in the morning, anywhere within your block that you care to. You may want to transect your block and cover it systematically, you may want to wander, you may want to survey by habitat. How you actually do it is up to you, as long as you make frequent visits to each habitat (preferably twice a week) throughout the breeding season. By making frequent observations in the same areas, you will be able to observe the birds during different stages of their breeding season. Birds originally listed as possible breeders early in the season may be upgraded to probable or confirmed birds as you make additional observations of breeding behavior. Birds are most active between five and eleven in the morning, and an hour's worth of observations during that time can yield good results.

The atlas information you receive should tell you the breeding season for your area. On the East Coast, June and July are considered the peak, varying a few weeks at either end as you travel north and south. But atlasing can be almost a year-round venture. Some species, notably the great horned owl, may be incubating eggs as early as January and February. Many species of hawks, owls, house sparrows, woodcock, mallards, Canada geese, common crows, and robins may begin nesting by March. In April, you should be looking for more owls, herons, nuthatches, pheasants, several woodpeckers, blackbirds, titmice, chickadees, and brown creepers, to name a few. May is the month of migrating and claiming territories, and the woods are virtually alive with birds. It is the busiest month of the year for a birder.

In June and July, things settle down, since the migrants are gone and what you will be seeing are most likely resident birds. You only need to determine if they are breeding, which brings to mind another point about atlasing. Too many birders tend to take things for granted—myself included—and atlasing can make you painfully aware of that fact. Case in point: the catbirds that were everywhere around my home. I saw them in the driveway, heard them calling from the bushes, caught them in the nets. Of course they are breeding here, I said to myself. But, when I had to verify that information via the data card, I could not seem to catch one in the act of holding territory, building a nest, carrying food, or doing any of the other things they were supposed to be doing. They were just there. My particular problem was solved by netting and banding a recent fledgling, but otherwise I would have been totally stymied.

There are a few species that breed late in the season. You also may have the opportunity to upgrade the breeding status of species that raise more than one brood.

Atlasers could take a rest in the fall, but when the leaves drop, you may want to get into your block and look for the used nests of hawks and owls. These birds often return to the same nest, and if you locate and note where they are now, you will still be able to find them in summer's foliage. If you notice a nest constructed mostly of leaves rather than sticks, it belongs to a squirrel, but make a notation to check it in January or February, since hawks and owls will sometimes use an abandoned squirrel's nest. (Now there's a question that just came to mind. Do hawks and owls "find" an abandoned squirrel's nest, or do they eat all the occupants and then take over?)

As you can see, atlasing tends to get you out into the field on a more regular basis, and during more seasons, than perhaps you normally would. Many birders fall into the "migration" rut, spending time in the field during spring and fall when birds are moving and there is a lot of action, and staying home when the warmer, quieter nesting season is in progress. It seems quiet by comparison to other times—territories have been established and males do not sing quite as loudly or as often, females are incubating, and when parents are feeding young, they approach their nests quietly and with caution—but there is plenty of action going on. You just have to look for it.

Another beneficial side effect of atlasing is that the program is forcing birders to get out into different locations. Many settle for known birding hot spots and fail to investigate the patch of woods in their own backyards. An examination of historical records (of New Jersey in particular) will yield the same locations listed time after time. These places may very well be excellent birding locations, but the atlas is proving that there are numerous others to be found.

Atlas projects are designed to be repeated at regular intervals of ten to fifteen years (or whatever figure seems necessary at the time), and then the results are compared against existing data. In this way, trends in breeding distribution, habitat availability, and other factors will be visible, and appropriate environmental actions can be implemented. If you have missed the atlas project in your state, plan to get involved the next time around!

For information about atlasing, contact: North American Ornithological Atlas Committee, Chandler S. Robbins, Migratory Bird and Habitat Research Laboratory, U.S. Fish and Wildlife Service, Laurel, MD 20708.

BREEDING BIRD SURVEY

This project is sponsored jointly by the U.S. Fish and Wildlife Service and the Canadian Wildlife Service. It attempts to detect and monitor the breeding populations of North American birds. Unlike the atlas, which concerns itself only with detecting the presence of breeding species, the BBS requires counting individuals sighted or heard.

Participants in the BBS are asked to choose a calm day in June to conduct the survey. Each volunteer is assigned a twenty-five-mile route. One half hour before sunrise, the observer begins his or her "run" by counting all birds seen or heard at the starting point during a three-minute period. This completed, the observer stops at half-mile intervals, listening, counting, and recording observations for three minutes, for forty-nine more stops. Only the results of the forty-nine stops and the starting point observations are counted as part of the survey.

Data from the BBS routes—more than 1,800 of them each year—are sent to the U.S. Fish and Wildlife Service in Laurel, Maryland, where they are reviewed by staff biologists and entered into the computers.

Breeding Bird Survey information is used in the preparation of environmental impact statements and for monitoring the status of individual species.

The BBS is open to anyone who wishes to participate, though there are a few basic requirements. Official observers must be familiar with bird songs and calls, since in the three minutes allotted to make the observations, many more birds will be heard than seen. Usually two BBS volunteers cover a route so it is possible for the beginner to accompany a more experienced birder.

For information, contact: Breeding Bird Survey, U.S. Fish and Wildlife Service, Laurel, MD 20708, or Canadian Wildlife Service, Ottawa, Ontario K1A 0E7.

BREEDING BIRD CENSUS

This survey, sponsored by the National Audubon Society and Cornell Laboratory of Ornithology, monitors the breeding populations of species within particular habitats. Unlike the predetermined block size of the atlas and the established route of the BBS, the Breeding Bird Census requires a minimum fifteen-acre study plot of a particular habitat. The base unit for a study plot is a hectare (2.471 acres).

Every detail of habitat within the study area is examined and logged. This includes the density and species of vegetation, available shrub cover, ground cover, species and size of trees, canopy height, water, and so forth. Additional information must include topography and elevations.

Once the study area has been carefully plotted the volunteer begins surveying the plot during the breeding season, making frequent visits to each habitat, and noting the presence of singing males (similar to the possible category of atlasing) and additional breeding evidence. Volunteers report their findings to the National Audubon Society.

For information, contact *American Birds*, National Audubon Society, 950 Third Avenue, New York, NY 10022.

NORTH AMERICAN NEST RECORD PROGRAM

The North American Nest Record Program (NRP) was initiated in 1965 by the Cornell Laboratory of Ornithology and the National Audubon Society. The NRP accepts both current and historical records, so if you have been keeping a journal and have notes about nesting observations you have made, you may want to contribute your information to the program.

Volunteers record nesting data on forms provided by Cornell. The form asks for information on the nest location, species, date of observation, clutch size, young, and so forth.

North American Nest Record forms are available to anyone interested in the program. Contact: NRP at Cornell Laboratory of Ornithology, 159 Sapsucker Woods Road, Ithaca, NY 14850.

CHRISTMAS BIRD COUNT

No mention of cooperative research projects can be complete without the Christmas Bird Count (CBC), probably the oldest organized project in the country. Sponsored by the National Audubon Society, the first CBC took place in 1900, with twenty-seven birders participating. Today, the CBC is conducted in all of the United States and Canada, all Central American countries, in northern portions of South America, and in the West Indies.

CBC volunteers count all birds observed within a fifteen-mile-diameter circle during one twenty-four-hour period. Individuals or groups of volunteers may survey within the same area, but circles cannot overlap. This is a popular activity for bird clubs, and it is also a good project for those armchair birders to participate in. Results of the count are published in *American Birds*. Contact: Christmas Bird Count, *American Birds*, National Audubon Society, 950 Third Avenue, New York, NY 10022.

FOUR

ORGANIZING
YOUR OWN PROJECT

Organizing Your Own Project

Now that we have covered the basic elements of field birding and have seen a sampling of established research projects, it is time to move on to something more original—the development of your own project.

Research is a harsh word, bringing to mind visions of antiseptic laboratories filled with white-coated scientists, but when applied to ornithology, research becomes a real blue-jeans job. Most of your time will be spent outdoors, in nature's laboratory, observing birds in their natural habitats.

There are so many things we still need to know—in virtually all areas of avian life—that there are more than enough worthwhile project possibilities available to keep us all busy for the rest of our natural lives.

Choosing a project will not be difficult. It should come naturally from an area of birding for which you have a special interest. Behavior. Nesting. Distribution. Migration. Habitats. Predation. Populations. Woodpeckers. These are just a few topics.

The beauty of organizing your own project is that you can tailor it to your needs. If you want to pursue it full time, so much the better. But if you are an amateur naturalist devoting a limited amount of spare time to birding, you can still achieve some worthwhile results, for yourself or to share with others. One of the most extensive studies of an individual species, for example, was conducted during an eight-year period by a housewife with several young children. As mentioned in Chapter 1, Margaret Morse Nice's *Studies in the Life History of the Song Sparrow* is a two-volume work (published in 1937 and 1943, respectively) that remains a classic in life-history study and is a model reference work used by today's ornithologists.

The idea for a research project begins with a question. Sit down with a pencil and paper and start listing questions you have about birds. It should not take you long to come up with a few dozen prospects. If you are working with a bander, he or she can probably supply you with additional ideas. If you have obtained your banding license, page through your banding manual. There are study suggestions listed there for many species, and there are specific questions that need answering. If you find yourself banding these species, you may have quite a few studies underway before long.

If you are still having difficulty deciding what you would like to do, consider examining historical birding journals to see if there is a study that could be conducted again for comparative analysis.

Before you begin, define the goal of your project. Your goal will depend upon a few factors. One of them will be an attempt to answer the question that prompted the study. This answer may never materialize. Most projects are really

A project need not be elaborate. Building birdhouses and observing nesting birds will provide hours of enjoyment.

designed for information gathering, to establish baseline data. If conclusions can be drawn from them, it's a bonus. At this stage, do not fret about conclusions. Concentrate instead on accumulating accurate, consistent information.

There are other equally important things to consider that may affect the way you approach your project. Who is the project for? Are you doing this largely for your own personal satisfaction? Do you intend to publish a paper in one of the professional journals? How much time will you devote to the work?

Since this book is dedicated to amateur naturalists, we will assume that your project, at least the first one, is intended primarily for your own enjoyment. Do not misunderstand. This is not to say your work should be any less important or the project itself taken less seriously.

As you have seen in previous chapters, the backbone of any research project is nothing more complicated than making regular observations and recording in detail everything that you see.

STUDYING BEHAVIOR

Since the study of behavior (ethology) will form the basis of any observations you make, you should have a working knowledge of the different types of behavior patterns, so that you can log them accordingly in your journals. The following does not represent all known behavior patterns, but it does briefly describe major categories.

Maintenance Behavior

These are the actions the bird takes to keep plumage in order. For the most part, these are inherited behavior patterns. The ones you most likely will see are:

PREENING. This is the bird's way of "combing" its feathers, removing dirt, and putting the individual barbs of the feather in order. It is accomplished by grasping the base of the feather in the beak and pulling the feather shaft and barbs through to the tip. It is usually accompanied by much feather fluffing and shaking and the striking of a few awkward poses for those hard to reach places.

OILING. Most birds are equipped with an oil gland at the base of the tail. The bird touches its beak, foot, head, or neck (depending on species) to the gland and then rubs the oil on the plumage. This is an important process for waterproofing feathers.

BATHING. Almost all birds will take a bath, but some species approach it with more enthusiasm than others. Ducks and geese really get into it, bathing while floating on the surface. They submerge head and neck, throwing the water over their backs, and they stir up a good shower by beating the surface with their wings. Songbirds are usually more discreet, wetting head and neck, and maybe squatting down into the water (usually a puddle) to flutter wings for a moment. They are very cautious, since soaked plumage impedes flight and leaves the bird more susceptible to dangers.

DUST BATHING. This is believed to have evolved among species of the desert where water for bathing is scarce. Dust bathing follows the same general procedure but substitutes dry, loose soil for water. This probably helps to rid the bird of ectoparasites. Not all species dust bathe.

SUNNING. This is often observed after bathing. The bird perches in the sun, spreads wing and tail, and enjoys. Birds also sunbathe after dust baths and preening.

ANTING. Anting is one of the more mysterious modes of maintenance behavior, and there is still much to be learned about it. There are two methods (each equally undesirable by human standards). Passive anting occurs when the bird positions itself amidst a colony of ants, relaxes wings and tail, and allows the ants to crawl into its plumage. During active anting, the bird picks up the ant in its beak and rubs it over the plumage.

Why birds indulge in such behavior is unclear, but it

seems to be a quest for the formic acid in the body of the ant. One theory suggests that the formic acid is an effective natural insect repellent. This is one area in need of further investigation.

FEATHER-SETTLING. This is often performed after any of the above maintenance behaviors. The bird raises its feathers and gives a vigorous shake.

STRETCHING. Stretching is often combined with feather settling. The bird stretches one wing and the corresponding leg toward the rear, or it extends both wings upward and backward.

Feeding Behavior

The feeding behavior of birds is directly related to their physical characteristics and the foods they eat. Some examples are:

PERCH FEEDING. This is hard to miss. The bird investigates the branch or shrub it is perched upon, picking up insects along the way.

CHISELING. Woodpeckers chisel or hammer at a tree, ripping away bark to expose insects hidden beneath it.

SCRATCHING. Sparrows and towhees scratch the ground, kicking aside the leaf litter to uncover food sources.

STOOPING. Practiced by falcons and other birds of prey, stooping is folding the wings and dropping at a high rate of speed to strike prey.

POUNCING. Hawks and owls employ this technique, waiting on a perch for movement below, then flying down rapidly to attack prey on the ground.

PLUNGING. Kingfishers and pelicans use this spectacular high-diving technique, plunging into the water from above to capture fish.

STALKING. Most readily observed in herons and egrets, stalking is a slow methodical walking stance to locate prey followed by a sudden stab.

Breeding Displays

Breeding displays are among the most fascinating behavioral displays you will ever have the pleasure of observing.

COURTSHIP DISPLAY. Courtship displays vary tremendously according to species. They can be short and to the point, lasting only a few moments at a time, or they can carry on all afternoon. I once was privileged to observe two flickers bobbing, bowing, calling, chasing, striking a pose (freezing), and displaying brightly colored undertails, for at least half an hour without a break.

Most courtship displays involve similar actions, usually on the part of the male attempting to attract the attentions of the female, but sometimes are practiced by both parties.

COURTSHIP FEEDING. Courtship feeding usually occurs after pairing and before nest building begins. The female behaves like a chick, calling to her mate by begging for food and fluttering her wings. He responds, naturally, by feeding her.

NEST BUILDING. This is most often a cooperative effort. Some species (especially the male house wren) build several nests before the female decides which one will be used. Other species search far and wide for just the right touch. Cliff and bank swallows add white feathers to their nests, great crested flycatchers must have a snakeskin in theirs, and many hawks add a fresh evergreen sprig.

INCUBATION. Eggs are incubated via a "brood patch" that develops on the breast of the bird. In species where this is a shared duty, both males and females will develop the patch. The incubating parent sheds a patch of feathers on its breast, and the area fills with blood and fluid. This area provides greater warmth to the eggs.

BROODING. After the eggs have hatched, the nestlings must be kept warm and shielded from the elements by the parent birds. This is accomplished by brooding. During cooler temperatures or inclement weather, the parent will settle over the nestlings as if incubating eggs. In warmer weather, the parent will shade nestlings by standing over them with wings outstretched.

DISTRACTION DISPLAY. Some species will do their best to distract a predator (or observer) by feigning injury and leading the predator away from nest and young. Killdeers will tempt a predator with a convincing "broken wings" display. Once, while walking through the woods with a friend, we upset a ruffed grouse with chicks. Acting instantly on a warning from the hen, the chicks scattered in all directions. The hen began to emit a mournful wailing sound, at the same time heading through the woods away from where her chicks were hidden, and making no effort to hide herself or her noisemaking. We did not follow her but continued on our way, circling around the spot where we knew her chicks were. The hen was making a wide circle that would eventually bring her back to her brood.

Social Behavior

The most obvious social behavior displays you will readily recognize are the aggressive or "agonistic" ones.

MOBBING. Mobbing behavior in birds serves more than one purpose and is usually associated with the presence of a predator. Mobbing begins when a predator is discovered—especially an owl trying to roost for the day in an area where there are nests and young of smaller birds—and the alarm is sounded. The alarmist is joined almost immediately by others of its kind and often by many other species that have nesting interests in the area. The mobbing birds will dive at the offending owl (or cat or person) in an attempt to drive it from their territory.

Crows are notorious for mobbing owls, and if a quiet summer day is disrupted by a mob of crows, investigate. You may be able to see the owl as the crows finally succeed in driving it from its roost. Crows will also mob hawks, and sometimes crows themselves are mobbed by smaller songbirds.

Other examples of aggressive behavior will be observed between birds holding nesting territories.

THREATENING. This action is designed as a bluff in some cases, and in others it is a force to be reckoned with. The threatening display of a great horned owl is impressive, to say the least. The owl fluffs its feathers to appear twice the size it really is, hisses, clacks its beak loudly, and presents its talons.

One of the best books I can recommend to you for the study of behavior is *A Guide to the Behavior of Common Birds, Volumes I and II*, by Donald W. Stokes. This book should be in the private library of everyone studying bird behavior.

Many of the methods you will use for your own project are basically the same as the ones previously discussed. You should keep a field notebook or journal and make regular, complete entries. Sketches are also helpful (they do not have to be works of art).

Let's assume you have decided to study the pair of house wrens you have just discovered nesting in the pantleg of your jeans on the clothesline. The birds are completing the nest, and you expect eggs to follow soon.

You may have missed gathering some information (you will want to check for it next year), or, if you have been keeping a journal, perhaps you already have some early observations recorded. When did the wrens arrive on the territory? Did the male arrive first? How soon after arrival did he establish the territory by singing? Did you notice more than one female responding? Did other males intrude on this territory? When did the female join the male? What type of courtship behavior have you observed? When were the first attempts at nest building started? Are there other nests in the territory built by the same pair? How many, and what is the location of each? Are there any other species showing an interest in these nests?

Since you are going to be spending the summer studying these wrens, why not do your homework? Create a "life-history data sheet" for the house wren. Go through your own collection of bird books, and then make a trip to the library and gather as much information about the wren as you can. Develop a standardized data sheet that can be used for any species.

LIFE-HISTORY DATA SHEET

AOU # _____

Species:_____

Confusing Species:_____

Scientific Name: _____

Description:_____

Preferred Habitat:_____

Summer Range:_____

Winter Range:_____

Spring Arrival Dates:_____

Fall Departure Dates:_____

Distinctive Habits:_____

Diet: _____

Courtship Behavior:_____

Nest Location:_____

Nest Materials:_____

Nest Measurements:_____

Number in Clutch:_____

Egg Dates:_____

Egg Description:_____

Incubation Period:_____

Number Broods:_____

Hatching Date(s):_____

Feeding Observations:_____

_____

Foods Offered Young:_____

Frequency:_____

Nestling Observations:_____

_____

Date(s) of Fledging:_____

Continued Parental Care:_____

Second Brood: (repeat above nesting information)

_____

Departure Dates:_____

Additional Notes:_____

This is just a suggested format. You may want to experiment with different forms until you find one to your liking. You may also want to include a picture, sketch or some other illustration. A loose-leaf format will allow you to add more notes as they accumulate.

Eventually, you should plan on preparing a life-history sheet for each bird you are likely to see as you pursue your birding habit. Researching the information will familiarize you with the vast array of bird books available and will help you remember important facts about each species. Writing the information on these forms will enforce in your mind what you have read, and it will make remembering easier.

Working on life histories is a pleasant way to enjoy birding when you cannot actually get out into the field, and when you are finished with them (you never really are), they are a valuable reference work in themselves.

Similar life-history data sheets were required of all volunteers at Raccoon Ridge—these included banding information as well as the information given in the above example. Whenever trainees were caught with an idle moment, Dot could be heard saying quietly, "How are you doing with your life histories?" At the time, when one wanted to be out in the field or otherwise actually *doing* something, sitting in the library poring through volumes of bird books seemed boring by comparison. But believe me, it is surprising how much you learn, and how much information you retain, by following such a simple procedure. Now I approach life-history data sheets with a different attitude, and I actually enjoy working on them (after ten years I am still not finished).

Similar information data sheets can be designed for habitat studies and other types of behavior studies. Experiment until you find one to suit your needs.

Making Observations

Throughout your study, you should attempt to observe what is happening at regular intervals. How often you make your observations will depend on how much time you have to devote to your study. This may be two or three times a week, once a day, at regular times throughout each day, or whatever. Consistency is important, however, and your observations will have more meaning if you establish a schedule and stick to it.

When observing the nesting behavior of any bird, do so with caution. Some species will desert their nests, particularly in the building or egg-laying stage, if they are disturbed. Others will desert even when incubation is well underway. Keep your visits to a minimum number, and do not linger at the nest site. Try not to disrupt the vegetation around or leading to a nest. Trampled vegetation and human scent leaves a well-marked trail for predators to follow. Check Chapter 3 for information on atlasing of nesting birds for alternate methods of observation.

Drawing Conclusions

As previously mentioned, finding an answer to the question that prompted your study may not be possible, even after you have accumulated an impressive file of observation documentation. What is usually missing is *quantity*, not of notes, but of subject matter. For example, if you spend the whole summer studying the pair of house wrens, you have accumulated a lot of valuable information about one pair of wrens. But based on your study, you may be tempted to say that wrens prefer to nest in old jeans. Among the possible nesting sites in your yard, the wrens *did* choose those old jeans. But what about the other wrens in that area? Unless you study *every* nesting pair of house wrens on your block, and find most of them nesting in old jeans, you cannot make that assumption. Also, you must consider the size of the study area, the habitat, and available food. Perhaps there is a surplus of old jeans in your neighborhood, but wrens twenty miles away prefer fence posts! It is important that your sampling size be large enough to support your conclusion, or no conclusion should be made.

Suggestions

As I mentioned in Chapter 1, you will most likely acquire all of the major field guides on the market today, and this will probably be followed by an assortment of bird books.

A library is an essential part of any research, and building your own collection of books will prove beneficial in many ways. It will definitely save time, you will have information you are seeking at your fingertips whenever you need it, and the classic bird books are always a sound investment.

In addition to a wide selection of general bird books at your local bookstore, more specialized volumes are always available by mail through the American Birding Association, National Audubon Society, National Wildlife Federation, Cornell Laboratory of Ornithology, and many other sources. Do not overlook garage sales and antiquarian bookstores for some real treasures.

Along with your book collection, you should begin to establish a "clippings" file. This will contain newspaper clippings, newsletters, articles, pictures, and similar material you collect from various sources. My files are arranged by AOU numbers, but you may want to group yours alphabetically by species, family, habitats—whatever works best for you.

A cross-reference system will be helpful in finding material. An article about the feeding habits of red-tailed hawks, for instance, might be filed under "AOU #337, Hawk, Red-tailed"; but I might also slip a note into the "Feeding Behavior" and "Predation" files as a reminder to check #337.

You will also want to subscribe to (and keep on file) the various professional journals and the many birding periodicals.

Collections

Collections are a useful educational tool. If you find yourself operating a nature center, bird observatory, or similar facility, you may wish to collect items for use in displays and as teaching aids. Making a collection can form the basis for a study in itself. *You will need to acquire the necessary government permits for keeping collections.* Write your state and federal fish and wildlife offices for applications.

NESTS. Nests should be collected *only* during the fall and winter months, when you are certain they are no longer being used. Check them carefully—a mouse or similar critter may have moved in after the birds vacated.

While collecting, carry pruning clippers, plastic bags, a notebook, tape measure, camera (optional), and field guides for identifying trees and shrubs. You can attempt to identify the nest itself when you get it home. Start by photographing the nest in its natural environment. Measure the height of the nest from the ground as best you can. Identify the tree or shrub it is in, and make any other general observations.

Some nests can be lifted from where they rest. You will find that others are firmly attached to a supporting branch, and in this case it may be necessary to clip the branches and take them also. Be careful not to unduly harm the tree or shrub. You could remove the nest from these branches later, but in doing so you will lose the fascinating detail of just how the bird managed to attach the nest to the branch in the first place.

Nests should be sprayed with an insecticide and sealed in a plastic bag for a few hours. This will eliminate any parasites that might be present. For long-term storage, use clear plastic boxes, glass cases, or plastic bags. Check them periodically for dampness or parasites that may have found their way to your collection. Mothballs always help.

Each nest in your collection should carry a tag bearing information as to date collected, location, species, and so forth. You also can place a numbered tag on the nest itself and keep the information in separate files (3 x 5 cards work well) coded with the numbered tags.

If you have more than one nest of a particular species (robin nests are easy to locate and collect), an interesting study is to dissect the nest and catalog the amount and different types of material used. This is a great project for children, too.

EGGS. The eggs of birds *should not be collected*. This was a very popular hobby during the 1800s, and the sheer numbers that were collected through the years are astonishing. It is a wonder most species survived. A few did not.

The only eggs you should even consider collecting are the bits and pieces of shells you may find during your nest collecting expeditions. All others are strictly out of the question. Egg collecting is illegal without a permit.

STUDY SKINS. People sometimes do not realize that a bird can be skinned and preserved using procedures similar to those used in preparing mammal skins. When done properly, feathers stay in place and retain their colors indefinitely. Do not go around killing birds in order to obtain skinning specimens! Road kills, window kills, rehabilitation failures, severe weather, winter kills—all of these birds can be used for study-skin purposes.

Most museums have a study-skin collection that is not on display to the general public but is available by special arrangement to those involved in research projects. Many of these museum collections are the product of early ornithology, when the shotgun was used as much as our field guides are used today.

Most bird observatories and some nature centers also maintain collections, and it is sometimes possible to borrow skins for a specific purpose.

Artists find them useful in studying the detail of feather placement and color. Banders use them to help with difficult identification of live birds in the hand. Children love them.

Learning to prepare skins is not difficult, but you will need a permit. A bird observatory or nature center should be able to tell you where you can receive training. Permit applications are available from the Fish and Wildlife Service.

PELLETS. Pellets of hawks and owls are relatively easy to collect (see Chapter 1). The pellets can be displayed in glass-topped boxes or clear plastic containers, or you may want to dissect a few and catalog the materials you find. From the bones, fur, teeth, and other ingredients in a pellet, you may be able to identify the prey species. Dissecting pellets is also a good learning activity for older children.

By now you can probably see that most projects are really very similar in the field methods they require. The best way to learn these is to do them. You will make some mistakes along the way—everybody does. Two of the biggest mistakes are taking too many things for granted, and therefore not recording enough detail about your observation, and not knowing when to stop. (Though I am not sure the latter can be considered a mistake.)

Suggestions for Field Studies

Here is a sampling of different ideas that might be considered for beginning field projects:

• A habitat study and bird survey of an area destined to be developed in the near future. This could be a few "vacant" acres of farmland at the edge of town due to become a housing development, or similar situation.

• A habitat study and bird survey of a parcel of recently logged woods. Compare what you find there with an undisturbed woods in the same area. Was the logging procedure necessarily harmful?

• Birding surveys in a new area. Find suitable habitat off the beaten "hot spot" tracks and survey what you find there.

• Discover a new hawkwatch lookout! Hawks migrate along mountain ridges during autumn, taking advantage of thermals. Well-known lookouts are jammed with as many birders as hawks passing overhead. Seek another vantage point and monitor the migration. You might make a discovery.

• Construct a floating blind in a swamp and monitor the birdlife you observe there. See *Wildlife Observer's Guidebook* listed in the Recommended Reading section of chapter 7 for floating blind information.

Use your imagination, and have fun.

FIVE

CARING FOR INJURED
AND ORPHANED BIRDS

Caring for Injured and Orphaned Birds

Most people who find themselves rehabilitating wild birds start off in the same manner—unexpectedly—and your initiation into this phase of ornithology will most likely follow the same pattern. For some people, rehabilitation is an inevitable side effect of the birding habit. Sometimes it is thrust upon you by a friend or neighbor (or a perfect stranger who heard somewhere of your birding interests), appearing at your door offering a featherless, half-dead baby on an outstretched palm, stammering something about how you know all about birds and will, of course, *do* something to save this one. Sometimes you initiate it yourself, when you are the one to discover a bird in trouble. Whatever the circumstances, you must make one of two choices: ignore the situation or take some type of rehabilitative action.

Most of the literature concerning the rescue and care of wildlife elaborates on the reasons why you should ignore the situation, and, in general, these reasons are quite valid.

Caring for distressed birds requires knowledge of diets, medical needs, and treatment of injuries, coupled with at least a working knowledge of a bird's natural development, behavior patterns, proper facilities, an acceptable release site, and a host of other specifics. This is knowledge the average person does not possess, and attempts at rescue, however well-intentioned, often end in disaster.

There is also the problem of people wanting to make pets of the wildlife they have successfully raised or nursed back to health. This is not only illegal but also can pose a serious threat to the health and welfare of both the animal and its captor.

To discourage the temptation to keep wildlife pets, and to discourage rehabilitation attempts by inexperienced persons, federal (and in many cases state) permits are required of anyone engaged in rehabilitation efforts. In addition, permit holders work in close cooperation with federal and state Fish and Wildlife agencies, must maintain accurate records, and submit annual reports accounting for the welfare and final disposition of each animal or bird they have taken under their care.

However justified the arguments *against* rehabilitation attempts may be, there are other factors that should be considered. First, with man's increasing encroachment and destruction of wild habitats, contact with displaced and distressed wildlife is inevitable. Pollution, pesticides, oil spills, out-of-control construction and the accompanying habitat destruction, high-tension wires, windows, cats, dogs, children, and automobiles are just a sampling of manmade hazards that have been responsible for bringing avian casualties and would-be rehabilitators together. In recent years, public concern for the conservation of wildlife has increased, and more people are actively expressing man's moral obligations in the matter.

A second point to consider is that, regardless of the discouraging statistics and literature concerning rehabilitation attempts, it is certainly not impossible for a person, armed with a little knowledge and a lot of effort, to successfully rehabilitate an injured or orphaned bird. Success may be the exception to the general rule, but it is within reach.

It is difficult at best to provide a complete treatise of wild-bird care in the space of one short chapter. The information provided here is intended to guide you through the basic treatment of the most common casualties, and to soften the surge of panic that will accompany the arrival of your first orphaned or injured bird. Keep in mind that you may be required to obtain the necessary permits from your state Fish and Wildlife office. Most important, realize from the start that the well-being of the bird will be your responsibility, and your goal is to see the bird released back into its natural habitat. Anything less is not successful rehabilitation.

Since baby birds are the most common casualties you will encounter, let's talk about their special requirements first. Before you can hope to successfully raise an orphaned bird, it is important to have at least a basic idea of a bird's natural development under normal circumstances. The following will be very basic in nature, and it is recommended that you take advantage of the publications listed in the Recommended Reading section, chapter 7, for more detailed information.

Newly hatched birds or "hatchlings" are known as nestlings until they are mature enough to leave the nest, at which time they become known as fledglings. Altricial young are featherless, blind, and completely helpless. They are confined to the nest until they are fully feathered and strong enough to fly (though some species will leave the nest before the skill of flying has been mastered). All passerines (perching birds and song birds) are altricial.

Precocial young are usually called chicks. They emerge from the egg covered with soft down, leave the nest soon after hatching, and are capable of feeding themselves within hours. Precocial chicks depend on the hen for protection and are never far from her side. Ducks and geese are examples of precocial birds.

To confuse matters, there are also semialtricial birds, which are covered with down upon hatching but are completely dependent on the parent birds (hawks and owls are semialtricial), and semiprecocial birds, which are down-covered and able to walk shortly after hatching but remain in the nest and depend on the parent birds for food and protection. The chicks of gulls and terns are examples of semiprecocial young.

Altricial nestlings and fledglings are the birds you will encounter most often. Let's look at their development more closely.

An altricial bird hatches from the egg looking like it should have spent a few more weeks on the inside. It is featherless, except for a few wisps of natal down. Bulging black eyes are tightly closed; the rubbery, swollen beak (usually bright yellow) is too big in proportion to the head and seems to have been added as an afterthought. The head itself is somehow supported by a spindly, wrinkled neck that looks like it will surely break under the strain. The wings are three sizes too small, the

A gentle tap under the beak will coax young raptors to accept food from human parents.

belly three sizes too big. The remains of the yolk and bodily functions are visible through transparent skin. Long legs and tangled feet are at the same time too large and too delicate. All in all, the newly hatched bird is not a pretty sight.

Happily, the youngster does not remain in this sorry state for long. A baby bird matures rapidly, and you will see physical improvements every day, so that in some species, the birds are fully feathered and ready to leave the nest within ten days of hatching. Timetables vary according to species. Generally, small-sized species and species that utilize an open nest develop at a much faster rate than larger species, or those that are cavity-nesters. For example, the young of most wood warblers will fledge in eight to twelve days of hatching; the young of nuthatches (small cavity nesters) in eighteen to twenty-one days; while the young of eagles may remain in the nest from seventy to eighty-four days.

In the wild, the parents will brood the young to keep them warm, and they will shade them from sun or rain by standing over them with wings outstretched. Usually both parents feed the young, beginning at sunrise and stopping at dusk. This averages out to a rotation feeding, with each chick receiving something to eat about every ten to fifteen minutes.

The key to successful rehabilitation is plain old common sense. Familiarize yourself with the type of parental care your orphan would receive under normal conditions and duplicate this care to the best of your ability. Sometimes your duplicated care may be something subtle, like shielding the orphans of cavity-nesting species from bright lights, simulating life in the nest hole. Sometimes it is more direct, such as cutting a mouse into bite-sized pieces for an orphaned owlet.

BEFORE YOU BEGIN— IS IT REALLY AN ORPHAN?

It is probably safe to say that at least half of the baby birds I have received in the past as orphans were not orphaned or abandoned at all. Most were newly fledged young that had not yet perfected their flying skills and were still, no doubt, under the care of their parents.

The discovery of a naked nestling is always a more serious problem, since it will not live long without food and protection from the elements, but taking the nestling home is not always the only solution.

In either case, returning the misplaced youngster to its nest is always the best possible form of rehabilitation. Unfortunately this is often easier said than done. A naked, helpless nestling discovered on the ground out in the open obviously did not get there of his own accord. If you (and the bird) are lucky, you need only to look above the nestling, into the eaves of the building, the branches of the tree, into the bushes or birdhouse in order to locate the nest the kid has fallen from. If you cannot locate the nest, the bird was probably dropped at the spot where you have found him by a nest-raiding bird, or perhaps a child, and in that case it will need rescuing.

If you can locate the nest, make every effort to put the baby back. The parent birds will not be upset because you have handled their youngster—birds have a poor sense of smell and they will not even notice. What if the whole nest has been destroyed or is in danger of falling? This sometimes happens to the nests of robins after a heavy rain—the mud used in the construction washes away. You can choose a substitute

Nestling and fledgling birds may only appear to be orphans. Be sure before you rescue.

nest, such as a small box, and wire it to the tree, as close to the original location as possible. Place the nestling in it, and *go away*. Watch from inside the house, or at least from a reasonable distance. The parents will not return to care for their young if you are too close.

Fledglings that are discovered on the ground do not always have broken wings. Again, these birds are in a normal, though hazardous stage of their development. Putting them back in the nest will not really help, since they will only jump out again. You can, however, place them in the branches of a nearby tree or bush, which will afford them some protection against predators and children. If you take the time to watch, from a reasonable distance, for an hour or more, you will most likely see the parent birds bringing the food. You need not do anything else.

Always, without exception, you should make every effort to return an uninjured, healthy youngster to its nest or parents. Rescue the bird only after you have determined that the bird will not survive without you, because the chances are very high that it will not survive with you, either.

Care of the Nestling

The first thing most nestling orphans will need in the way of first-aid treatment is warmth. This is especially true if the orphan is newly hatched and still featherless. At this stage, songbirds are essentially cold-blooded, and their bodies adjust to the temperature of the surrounding air. Body temperature control does not develop until five to six days from hatching in many species. A chilled baby will be listless, will feel cool to the touch, and will make little or no effort to beg or "gape" for food. You can use your own body heat to warm the baby by placing it under your shirt, against your skin, or simply cupping it gently in your hands. (It is useless to attempt to feed a chilled baby; in fact, you can kill it, so getting the youngster warm is always your first concern.)

Once you have warmed the baby in this manner, you must provide a substitute nest and a more permanent source of heat. Line a small bowl, basket, or similar container with fifteen or twenty tissues, place the nestling inside, and cover with another tissue to protect from drafts. Place the "nest" on a towel-wrapped heating pad set on low, or suspend a 60-watt light bulb about twelve inches above it. Some people use hot water bottles, but this can result in inconsistent temperatures as the water cools if not closely maintained. In any case, keep a thermometer on hand to monitor the temperature. You want to keep the bird warm; you don't want to cook it. For a featherless nestling, it should be around 95 degrees Fahrenheit. A lightly feathered orphan should be kept in an environment at 80 degrees Fahrenheit, and one that is fully feathered will probably need no supplemental heat source unless it is sick or injured. Soak a sponge in water and keep it next to the nest to provide some humidity.

Using this method, it will be very easy to keep your youngster clean. Simply remove the soiled tissue on top of the pile and add a few more when needed. Avoid the temptation to use a real nest, since these often carry parasites and are much more difficult to keep clean. You are going to be in for a lot of work as it is, and you will find using the tissues to be much more convenient.

Now that your orphan is warm and comfortable, you can think about the next priority—food. In the wild, the youngster would be fed a wide variety of high-protein foods: insects, worms, grubs, and similar creatures. Considering the fact that you will be feeding this bird every ten minutes or so, and that you might possibly be raising more than one orphan at the same time, some quick calculations on your part will demonstrate the odds against your being able to collect enough insects to do the job. This will be one area where you will have to alter your duplicated care techniques for a more convenient system, but the importance of a protein-rich, balanced diet cannot be sacrificed in the process.

There is a convenient alternative. Young songbirds respond well to a diet of soft dog food, supplemented with natural foods as the bird matures. You may use any one of the kibbled varieties, provided you soak it in water until soft, or you may use one of the canned varieties. I find the kibble easier because I can mix a fresh batch when I need it, instead of being faced with a whole can of food that can spoil easily in warm weather. The soaked kibble does not fall apart when I am trying to feed it, as the canned food will do, and the kibbled pieces are "bite-size" for many birds.

The dog food diet works well on all songbirds (seed eaters included), woodpeckers, swifts, and similar insect-eating species. If fussing makes you feel better, you can also prepare bits of hard-boiled egg yolk, pieces of lean beef, raw beef kidney, insects, mealworms, maggots, and earthworms. *Do not* feed bread soaked in milk, which for some reason seems to be a popular offering among well-meaning rescuers. Remember the common sense mentioned earlier? Where does a wild bird obtain milk to feed her young, and why would she want to, since birds are not mammals? Milk is actually difficult for most birds to digest, and while it may not kill your orphan outright, it can certainly cause him a few digestive problems.

As soon as you know what species of bird you are raising (you may have to wait for some feathers for this), and your orphan is eating well, begin to supplement the dog food diet with some of the natural foods the bird would receive in the wild, if at all possible. You can also offer fruit—blueberries, strawberries, cherries, and grapes are always favorites. Consult the Recommended Reading section for this chapter (located in chapter 7) for more information on diets and feeding.

If your orphan is warm and comfortable, coaxing it to eat should not be difficult unless the youngster is near death. You may have to force feed a very weak nestling until it regains its strength. To force feed, gently press against the side of the beak at the back portion, open the bird's mouth, and place the food well down the throat. Be careful not to exert too much pressure on the rubbery beak, since you can easily damage it and cause it to mature deformed.

If you are having difficulty opening the beak of a very weak nestling, you can try the "drop" method. Add water to the food until it is the consistency of thick soup. Dip the end of a toothpick or similar tool into the food and allow it to collect at the tip. Hold the bird and allow the food to "drop" into the crack where the upper and lower mandibles (beak) come together. The bird should make an attempt to swallow the liquid. Continue feeding in this manner until the bird shakes his head, slinging food all over the place and indicating he has had enough.

A healthy nestling will eagerly open its mouth wide, or gape, as soon as you tap the edge of the "nest." This simulates the parent bird's arrival on the nest. When the nestling's eyes are open and it recognizes you as its food source, you will not be able to come near without setting off a display of wing-fluttering, gaping, and "feed me" calls.

If you have ever watched a parent bird feed its young, you probably noticed that the food is unceremoniously stuffed down the nestling's throat. Your method of feeding must closely match the action of the parent. A young bird cannot swallow unless the food is placed well down in the throat, behind the tongue, and this is where many people run into trouble. They timidly place a bit of food in the baby's mouth, and wonder why it just sits there or continues to gape with a mouth full of food. Use your fingers, a pair of tweezers, a toothpick, or similar tools if necessary—if you use anything but your fingers be gentle—but be firm and get that food down the throat.

A very small nestling may only take one piece of food at a feeding, while larger, older birds may accept upwards of ten pieces at a session. The important thing is to feed the baby as much as it will accept. You cannot overfeed a baby bird that begs for food; it will simply refuse to gape and go to sleep when it has had enough, but you can easily starve one in a matter of hours with inadequate feedings. Force feeding is another matter, and you must exercise caution not to overfeed and suffocate the bird.

You should offer food whenever the bird calls for it, or at least every fifteen minutes or so at first. As the bird gets older, the time between feedings will lengthen, so that you are feeding a fledgling about every half hour to forty-five minutes.

Avoid giving the bird water until it fledges and can take the water on its own. It is too easy to accidentally introduce water into the lungs when placing water in a bird's mouth, and the bird will receive enough moisture from the food.

Until the bird fledges, there isn't much more in the way of care that you must provide other than keeping the orphan warm and protected from the family cat, dog, and very small children.

Care of the Fledgling

The day will come when your orphan will hop up on the edge of its nest to have a look around. This is the first step towards fledging, and from this point forward it is a good idea to put nest and bird inside a spacious cage. The bird may spend a few days just perching on the edge of the nest, but sooner or later, and usually without much warning, it is going to jump. This can be disastrous if the nest is left unattended on a table and the fledgling jumps over the side, since this stage of development often takes place before the bird is capable of flying. It is one thing to leap out of a nest and crash-land on Mother Earth; it is quite another to make sudden contact with a hardwood floor.

The cage should provide enough room for the fledgling to move around without injuring itself. Be sure there are one or two sturdy perches within easy reach of the nest. Once the bird fledges you can remove the nest—he will not return to it. You should now put down a small dish of food and a shallow dish of water, large enough to accommodate a bath. A pie plate works nicely; add a flat stone in the water for added security.

Until now your orphan has been accustomed to your stuffing the food down its throat, but you should soon notice a change in feeding behavior. The bird will show more curiosity toward the food you are offering, and it is now time to alter your feeding methods. Instead of automatically stuffing the food, give the fledgling the chance to take it from you. Hold the food in front of its beak, within easy reach. The bird will gape and beg as usual, but it will probably make no attempt to take the food, even though it is right under its nose. After a few seconds, feed the fledgling in the usual manner.

The bird will be spending more and more time exploring its surroundings, pecking at perches, the dishes of food and water, the cage bottom and sides, and sometimes its own toes. Eventually this exploratory behavior will carry over to feeding, and one day the bird will make a half-hearted stab at the food you are holding before its beak.

When the bird finally does grab the food in its beak all by itself, it most likely will not know what to do with it. This is a new experience, and it may stand there holding the food in the tip of its beak, making no attempt to swallow. Be patient; eventually it will get the hang of it and begin to feed itself.

Since these first feedings tend to be haphazard at best, you should continue feeding the bird in the accustomed fashion until you are absolutely certain the bird is capable of feeding well on its own. Even then, it will continue to gape for food whenever it can. Parent birds continue to feed their young after fledging, ensuring survival while the birds learn to fend for themselves.

The ability to fly is inherited, but coordination and strength require much practice, and your fledgling must be given the opportunity to perfect its flying skills before it can be released. A large indoor or outdoor flight pen is the ideal accommodation, but unless you plan to make rehabilitation a major part of your birding habit, such a pen is probably not practical. An enclosed porch, greenhouse, or similar structure will also serve the purpose, or, if all else fails, a room in your home (this could be messy). The major requirement for your flight area is that it be safe from cats and other predators. It should also prevent the fledgling from escaping prematurely. You should remove anything the bird could accidentally (or purposely) destroy. One northern oriole fledgling I left flying free in my living room spent one afternoon methodically lacerating the leaves on twenty-six African violet plants. If you must keep the fledgling caged, be sure that it receives a few hours flying time each day.

If you have raised this bird indoors, begin now to "weather" it by placing the cage outside during the daylight hours and gradually working toward leaving it outdoors overnight. Be sure the cage is out of the reach of cats, raccoons, and other dangers and is protected from the elements.

If at all possible, your fledgling should be banded (see Chapter 2). The recovery of a banded, hand-raised bird will provide some valuable insight to the success or failure of any rehabilitation project.

Release

Once your bird is flying well, is capable of feeding itself (even though it prefers to be fed), and is reasonably adjusted to the outdoors, it is time to begin the final phase of rehabilitation and the goal of the whole project: release. Plan to release the bird when two or three days of fair weather conditions are forecast. Early in the morning, open the cage door. Secure the door in the opened position so the fledgling can return at will. Provide fresh food and water either inside the cage, or nearby it, where the fledgling can locate it easily.

Most likely, the fledgling will not venture too far from "home" in the beginning, but this will vary with species. Cedar waxwings, for example, travel great distances as fledglings and will disappear shortly after their release. Robins will return to you for at least a week, and you will begin to wonder if blue jays and orioles will ever leave.

Before you decide that you have a fledgling that is hopelessly "imprinted," be sure you have allowed ample time under the right conditions for the bird to make the adjustment.

Imprinting normally occurs soon after hatching. It is the way an infant bird identifies itself as belonging to its parents. When humans are foster parents, birds can become imprinted on them. The result is a bird that attaches itself to humans. The degree of imprinting varies with species, but in most cases it can be avoided, outgrown, or the bird can be retrained.

One particular blue jay that comes to mind was nearly kept in captivity as an incurably imprinted bird, even though "Blue" had been officially banded and released for several weeks. The bird would disappear for hours at a time but would arrive like clockwork at the back door of the YMCA camp's dining hall at mealtime. He showed no fear of anyone, and we never observed him hanging around with other blue jays. We were considering holding him over the winter when, well into the fall migration, he failed to return.

We feared the worst and wondered if he had made it, and then we received a banding report. It seems our Blue was alive and well, recaptured by a bander in Connecticut. As if to keep in touch with us, Blue managed to get himself caught a few weeks later in South Carolina, and again in a third location that escapes me now. There are two points to that story: Get your rehabilitated birds banded if possible, and be sure you have allowed ample time under the right conditions for the bird to make the adjustment. Certainly this is an area where more research is needed.

When you do determine an individual is unfit for release, either by virtue of its being incurably imprinted or through a physical disability, you can usually find a nature center, wildlife refuge, or similar facility where the bird will be welcomed as part of the educational staff. However, if you raise your orphan in the manner described in this chapter, avoid unnecessary handling, and allow ample time for adjustment, you should not encounter this type of problem very often.

Birds Requiring Special Care

It is obvious that not all species can be raised according to the methods discussed thus far. While all species require specific diets and housing, some are decidedly more difficult to care for than others. You would not be able (nor would you want to) raise a great blue heron in your living room. The following species are the most common difficult species you will encounter. Do not attempt to care for these birds unless you can provide the specialized diets, housing, and release techniques they demand.

HAWKS AND OWLS. These birds require a balanced diet of fresh meat, with bones, fur, hair and feathers included. In the wild, they obtain this by killing and eating other birds and animals. Hawks usually tear chunks of meat and bone from their prey, while owls tend to swallow their prey whole. In either case, whatever material their bodies do not use (bones, fur, feathers) is regurgitated later in the form of a pellet. The bones, fur, feathers, and such serve as roughage and keep the digestive system functioning properly.

The feeding requirements of raptorial birds are the reason for placing them in this "special care" section. While most people have no problem mixing up a batch of dog food for the robin, some do tend to balk when it comes to cutting a mouse into bite-size pieces. In fact, we sometimes used this technique at RRBO to persuade would-be "rescuers" to surrender a raptor chick to a rehabilitation center.

Quite often we would receive calls from people who had orphaned hawk or owl chicks in their possession and were calling for information on how to care for the birds, which they thought "would be fun to raise." After lengthy conversations about wildlife pets, the law, retraining the birds for life in the wild, and the other responsibilities associated with caring for such a bird, most people had a better understanding and surrendered the bird to a qualified center.

There are always a few exceptions, and one particular incident sticks in my mind. The caller was determined to keep the screech owl her son had found in the woods. Dot can be equally determined, especially when the welfare of a bird is at stake. After speaking to the caller on the phone, it was apparent to Dot that this woman did not have the knowledge (or the

As a raptor chick matures, it can be encouraged to pick up its food by touching the meat to the bird's talons. Hunting skills must be learned and perfected before release.

common sense) necessary to successfully raise the bird. But the woman was persistent. "Just tell me what to feed it, and it'll be all right."

"Do you have a blender?" Dot asked sweetly.

"Yes."

"Fine. What you need to do is catch at least two mice a day. Put them in the blender and chop. . . ." The bird was delivered to the rehabilitation center within half an hour.

Actually there is truth in the blender technique. Newly hatched raptors respond best to a mouse that has been crushed to a mushy consistency. In an emergency situation, you can feed strips of lean beef, beef heart, or chicken parts, but this should be only on a temporary basis until the bird can be brought to a qualified facility. Maintaining a supply of mice can create additional problems, since a full-grown hawk or owl may consume as many as ten mice a day. Established raptor rehabilitation centers sometimes obtain the healthy "control" mice from research laboratories. These are kept frozen and thawed and warmed as needed. Some also obtain day-old chicks from poultry and gamebird farms to supplement the rodent diet. Fresh road kills also provide additional food sources.

Unlike the passerine birds discussed earlier that learn to feed themselves easily, raptors must practice their hunting techniques, and master them before they starve to death. The killing instinct is inherited, but the skill required to accomplish it must be learned.

For a bird raised in captivity, this presents still more

problems. You must be absolutely certain the bird is capable of feeding itself before it is released, and there is a vast difference between the half-tame, plodding, domesticated mouse you might raise for the purpose, and the wild, ever-alert lightning-fast mouse the bird will depend on as prey.

Raptor rehabilitation facilities are equipped with specialized flight cages, allowing the birds room to develop their hunting skills. There are also specially designed holding pens that allow the bird to be raised with minimal human contact, reducing the effects of imprinting. Since raptors mature more slowly, it is sometimes necessary to hold the birds through the first winter to ensure their survival.

With all of the above considerations in mind, there still may be an occasion where you find yourself with a raptorial chick in need of immediate care. Until you can contact a qualified rehabilitation center, the following guidelines should be followed.

Raptor nestlings should be kept warm and free from drafts. An extra source of heat is unnecessary (since the chick is down-covered) unless the chick is debilitated.

Feeding methods are slightly different. Raptor chicks do not gape as vigorously as passerine birds. They can be stimulated to pick up their own food by touching it to their feet.

You may need to force-feed the raptor chick the first few times until the bird realizes you are offering food. To force-feed a raptor, use your fingers, tweezers, chopstick, or similar tool. Press the meat gently to the side and back part of the beak. When it opens, gently push the meat to the back of the throat. The bird will swallow and, after a few similar feedings, will begin to take the meat. Since raptors chicks do not gape as readily as passerine nestlings do, it may be necessary to palpate the bird's crop to determine if the feeding is sufficient. The crop should feel "padded"—not stuffed! In any case, stop feeding if the chick begins to regurgitate. Chicks under two weeks of age should be offered food about every hour. Extend feeding intervals to two hours for chicks two to three weeks of age. At four weeks, feeding should be spaced four hours apart and remain so until the bird is fully feathered and fledged. At this point, gradually extend the time between feedings until the bird is receiving one meal a day.

Again, hawks and owls should be referred to a qualified rehabilitation center as quickly as possible. If you are particularly interested in this area of rehabilitation work, you may want to volunteer some time with an established center.

WATERFOWL AND WADING BIRDS. These species are very difficult to care for properly unless you can offer the water for swimming, wading, and feeding that they will require. In an emergency situation you can use a child's plastic swimming pool or your bathtub.

I once cared for a Peking duck that had been attacked by a dog. It was late in January, and, because I lacked proper outdoor facilities in the dead of winter, the duck lived in a large box in the bathroom (luckily I had a huge bathroom) while his wounds healed, enjoying daily duck-time in the tub. My son called him Donald, and Donald soon became quite possessive of the bathroom, quacking in protest when his "territory" was invaded. It was almost worth having a duck in the bathroom to see the reaction of unsuspecting guests who tried to discreetly use the facilities and instead had their intentions loudly publicized by a quacking duck. Anyway, Donald fared quite well under these circumstances, and one morning in March, after much fussing and quacking, presented us with an egg. We had fresh duck eggs for the next few weeks, until the ice broke up on the ponds and "Ms." Donald was released.

Ducks and geese can be fed a mixture of grain, cracked corn, dog food, or uncooked oatmeal, but other species are considerably more difficult to house and feed properly. Many fish-eating birds require force feeding, which can be a two-man job. These birds will also regurgitate their meals if upset, and if you think the fried fish smell from last night's dinner causes an odor problem in your kitchen, consider the effects of a regurgitated mackerel. Herons can be quite dangerous to handle—they will stab at you with their spearlike bills, aiming for your eyes.

If you must care for a heron or similar bird until you can locate a rehabilitation center, keep the bird in a large, covered cardboard carton (ask your local appliance store for a refrigerator or stove box). Place a large basin or bucket of fresh water—weighted with rocks so it will not tip easily—in a corner of the box and disturb the bird as little as possible. Remove the water when you are ready to transport the bird to the rehab center.

If you will be feeding the bird during the time you are holding it, try to obtain some live baitfish from the local sportshop, drop them in the water bucket, and leave the bird alone. Few birds will attempt to eat while you are watching. When live fish are unavailable, you can defrost a frozen fish and swirl it around in the water so it appears to be moving.

I do recommend that you contact a rehabilitation center or your local Fish and Wildlife office immediately when dealing with these species.

PRECOCIAL CHICKS. These birds are probably among the easiest ones to care for, if for no other reason than they will feed themselves. They will require an enclosed area where they are free to roam about, yet are protected from predators. A 25-watt light bulb suspended in the corner of the pen (for very young chicks, a large cardboard box is sufficient) will provide an adequate source of heat.

Provide the chicks with commercially sold chicken mash, supplemented with insects, earthworms, mealworms, crickets, and similar creatures. Supply also a shallow dish containing grit—commercially sold parakeet grit will serve the purpose. As the chicks mature, the cage should be placed outdoors, but only if the chicks are sheltered and have access to grass and soil.

You may need to teach the chicks to eat. In the wild, the hen teaches her young by "talking" to them, picking up seeds, and dropping them in front of the young. By imitating their mother, the chicks soon learn to peck for their own food. If you can "talk" to the chicks in their own language, great, but more than likely you will have to teach them by demonstrating. Pick up some food and drop it in front of the chick to get its attention. It should respond by pecking at the food you have dropped. Another technique is to tap the floor of the box lightly with your finger or a toothpick in a pecking motion.

If you are certain your charges are not feeding themselves, you may need to use the drop-feeding technique explained earlier.

PIGEONS AND DOVES. These birds do not gape for food, as do the young of altricial birds described earlier. Instead, they are fed by taking a liquid secretion (pigeon milk) from the crop of the parent bird. As a substitute, you can use cooked wheat cereal mixed with an equal amount of water until soupy. Cut the tip off the nipple of a doll baby bottle, fill it with formula, and offer the cut off end to the baby. It will insert its beak into the "soup" and feed. Repeat feedings about every hour.

INJURED BIRDS

Most of the common injuries of passerine birds can be successfully treated by the combined efforts of a veterinarian and the amateur birder. Veterinarians are sometimes skittish about handling wild birds, but the vet's medical skill coupled with your practical birding knowledge and willingness to help will result in an effective team.

It is impossible to detail the treatment of various injuries in this limited space. The following are suggested guidelines for first-aid treatment, and they should be regarded as such. For more detailed information, consult the books recommended for this chapter in chapter 7.

More often than not, treatment of fright and shock are more urgent than treating the wound itself (an exception, of course, is heavy bleeding). Upon receiving an injured bird, you should place it in a covered box or similar container and keep it warm and quiet, especially if the bird has just traveled halfway across town in the back seat of the car with three kids and the family dog.

An hour in the box will do more to stabilize its condition

than any other immediate treatment you can offer. Sometimes, this is the only treatment necessary if, say, the bird has collided with a window. If you suspect there are no injuries other than shock, the bird should be released as quickly upon recovery from the shock as possible.

Broken bones require special care, especially if the skin is punctured. A vulnerable part of a bird's wing, and almost impossible to visually detect, is the "wrist." This is the tip portion of the wing and, in a small bird, may be diagnosed by the bird's inability to gain altitude. Easier to see are breaks of the larger bones in the wing. The affected wing will hang lower than the healthy one. A bird with a hanging wing, however, may have problems with the leg, which throws the bird off balance and makes it appear like one wing is lower than the other. If you are not sure what the problem is, consult a veterinarian.

Not all wing and leg breaks require splinting, especially on the smaller species. The break will usually heal well without a splint, provided the bird is kept warm, quiet, and well fed. A bird is a perfectly balanced creature, and the added weight of a splint sometimes causes more stress and potential problems than it cures. Sometimes, in place of a splint, I will use a very lightweight tape, such as the pink hair-setting tape sold in the cosmetic section of the supermarket. This works well for immobilizing a delicate wingtip and, because it is designed to be easily removed from human hair, is also easily removed from feathers.

Of course there are times when a splint is essential. You should always consult your veterinarian, since a poorly placed splint will do more harm than good. The best splinting methods sometimes need to be invented, according to the injury and the patient.

Any splint will disrupt a bird's balance, and you may need to compensate for this. One duck with broken wings that comes to mind was splinted by the veterinarian. It was a beautiful job and everything looked fine, except that the duck, with wings splinted and wrapped, could not balance and tended to fall forward on his face. The veterinarian, accustomed to inventing and compensating where wildlife was concerned, added a wrap of tape around the duck's tail. He then added small metal weights to the tape until the duck was in balance and taped them in place. The result was a very heavy, slow-moving duck, but the improvisation worked, the wing healed, and the bird was released in fine condition.

Broken legs are somewhat easier to splint, especially if the break is a clean one of the tarsus. A plastic soda straw, cut to the proper length, split lengthwise, and placed around the tarsus, can be secured to the leg at each end with a small piece of surgical or cosmetic tape.

A bird that is bleeding from a wound needs immediate help. Since the blood volume of a bird comprises between ten and fifteen percent of its total body weight, and higher in small and baby birds, a bird does not have much blood to spare. Nature has compensated to an extent by making avian blood quick to clot, so that excessive bleeding usually does not last too long. You can aid in the clotting procedure by using a styptic pencil.

Birds suffering from cat attacks may not exhibit readily visible signs of injury. The puncture wounds from predator fangs and claws may not bleed excessively and may be hidden

A simple but effective cast can be made from a plastic soda straw, split lengthwise and taped lightly around a fractured tarsus.

in the feathers. You should consult a veterinarian if you suspect the bird has been mauled by a cat.

Recently, aviculturists have discovered (and are still investigating) that an acute *Pasteurella bacteremia* circulates in a bird's blood following a cat attack, concentrating in major organs and resulting in death within seventy-two hours of the attack. This condition was at first believed to be caused by an allergic reaction to some element in the saliva of the cat. It also has been determined that the degree of seriousness of the attack does not affect the condition—birds with minor scratches and puncture wounds are just as susceptible as birds with major injuries. The infection can be treated with aminoglycoside, steroids, and ampicillin (by the veterinarian), but speed is of the utmost importance.

Oiled Birds

We are taught in science class that oil and water do not mix, but many of us fail to realize that oil and birds do not mix either. Oil is deadly to a bird, be it a thorough soaking from a major oil spill or a few spots of freshly applied road tar stuck on a foot or feather.

Birds that are not heavily oil-soaked are still in grave danger, since they will attempt to clean the offensive elements from their feathers and feet by preening. In the process, the oil will be ingested, and what follows is not difficult to figure out.

Oiled birds are not always victims of spills. I have encountered birds caught in flypaper and in the commercially sold tacky product smeared on the base of a post feeder, intended to repel squirrels. Birds also come into contact with creosote applied to fences and similar concoctions brushed on trees during the gypsy moth wars, and freshly oiled or tarred roadways.

During the late 1970s the Humane Society of the United States (HSUS) played an important part in the rescue of birds during a 500,000-gallon crude oil spill in Chesapeake Bay that affected about 15,000 birds.

The combined efforts of HSUS personnel, the Coast Guard, Fish and Wildlife Service, assorted bird rescue organizations, and volunteers resulted in what proved to be the most successful on-site bird rescue operation in history. One out of every three birds was saved. That may not sound so good, but given the devastating effects of a major spill, it is extraordinary.

Prior to this spill, there was virtually no organized method of rescuing and treating oiled birds, and most of them perished. The Fish and Wildlife Service and the Coast Guard, in cooperation with HSUS, the International Bird Rescue Research Center in California, and community animal welfare agencies, began to sponsor oiled-bird training seminars. The seminars were open to anyone interested in volunteering to help rescue oiled birds in the event of a spill. The seminars offered practical training in the capture, treatment, and release of the birds and resulted in teams of organized volunteers being "on call" and ready to mobilize quickly when a spill occurred.

The basics of cleaning an oiled bird are the same, no matter what type of oil is involved. The birds are usually given a rehydrating solution to help stabilize their condition. Beaks are taped, or the bird is enclosed in a "body sack," a pillowcase or similar covering, to prevent the bird from attempting to clean the plumage and thus ingesting the oil. They are kept warm and quiet and no attempt to clean them is made until their condition is stabilized. Warmth is important; hypothermia is one of the biggest causes of death, since oil-soaked feathers are useless insulators.

When a bird is ready for cleaning, it receives a series of warm-water baths. Mild detergents are used to scrub the oil from feathers. The bird is bathed as many times as necessary to remove the oil. After bathing and rinsing, birds are dried thoroughly with warm-air blowers. They are closely monitored for signs of illness or stress. They are kept warm, allowed to rest and recover from the bathing ordeal, and are then fed.

The birds also receive swim therapy, which allows them to restore the natural waterproofing to their feathers. Rescued birds are banded prior to release.

If you are interested in learning more about the care of oiled birds, contact your state chapter of the HSUS or your Fish and Wildlife office.

POISONING AND DISEASES

Many avian diseases are difficult to diagnose and treat without the aid of a veterinarian. You will encounter more injuries than diseases; because of their rapid metabolism, a bird that contracts a serious disease usually does not live long enough to be rescued in the first place.

The most frequently encountered problems are usually the result of chemical poisoning from insecticides, such as those used for the control of gypsy moths. Many species feed on gypsy moth caterpillars and are, in turn, fatally poisoned by the pesticides.

Birds are also susceptible to food poisoning, which most commonly occurs when discarded seed and feces are allowed to accumulate under feeders. To prevent this, the soil under feeders should be periodically removed (to a depth of about three inches) and replaced with clean soil.

Because of the complexity of the subject, the best recourse in dealing with these and other avian ailments is experience, coupled with a good reference library and the services of your veterinarian. Consult the books recommended for this chapter for additional information.

Questions are frequently raised about the transmission of wildlife disease to humans. Very few avian diseases can be transmitted to people, but always use basic common sense and cleanliness when handling any wildlife.

Rabies is probably the most familiar disease associated with wild animals. It is a viral disease of the nervous system, transmitted by introducing the virus to open cuts or scratches in the skin by way of mucous membranes. The most common occurrence, therefore, is through the bite of an infected animal. It is a disease peculiar only to mammals. *Birds cannot get or transmit rabies.* Any mammal, however, is susceptible to the disease, though certain species seem to be more easily affected. Among these are raccoons, skunks, and foxes.

A more serious concern of avian rehabilitators is tetanus, another disease contracted through an open wound. It is highly recommended that anyone working with wildlife—including birds—keep their tetanus inoculations up to date. This is especially true if you will be handling hawks and owls, the species most capable of inflicting such a wound.

KEEPING RECORDS

The importance of keeping accurate records of your wildlife rehabilitation efforts cannot be overemphasized. If you obtain government permits to care for wildlife, you will be required to submit an annual report on the birds and animals you handle, and consulting accurate records will make this task easier.

The need for recording what you are doing runs deeper than filing reports. Rehabilitation is a relatively new area of bird study, and each case is a learning experience. By documenting your successes and failures, you will be building valuable references for yourself and for colleagues in the field.

The bulk of this chapter has dealt with the care of injured and orphaned birds, but now we should take a moment to talk about you, the rehabilitator.

Caring for injured and orphaned animals is not for everyone. You will probably experience more failures than you care to admit, and you will often wonder if you have done the right thing. If it is any consolation, you should know that, statistically, rehabilitation is still considered to be successful when you have a less than fifty percent success ratio. Your efforts to raise a wild orphan are roughly equivalent to the efforts of a duck in raising a human baby. Pretty frightening, huh? Granted, humans have the gift of superior intelligence and all that we have created to go with it, but when you get right down to it, you are human and a duck is a duck. We do the best we can under the circumstances, and we are thrilled when it works. When it does not, and the bird or animal you have poured your heart and soul into saving dies in your hands, accept it. Try to learn something helpful from the experience that you can apply to the next case. You will soon find that each one will become a little easier and more successful.

You also may wish to become a member of the National Wildlife Rehabilitation Association (NWRA), which is an organization primarily structured for active rehabilitators. The NWRA conducts annual symposiums, publishes a newsletter and membership directory, and can provide information and services for rehabilitators with specific problems. For information, contact: National Wildlife Rehabilitation Association, 708 Riverside Avenue South, Sartell, MN 56377-1520.

SIX

AVICULTURE

Aviculture

The subject of aviculture, the hobby of keeping caged birds, is not one that is normally covered in books about wild birds. Birders and naturalists seem to abhor the idea of keeping birds as pets, sometimes blaming aviculturists for endangering the welfare and, in some cases, the very existence of exotic species by creating and promoting a market for them.

Actually, birders and aviculturists are not so different from each other—in fact, most aviculturists are also avid birders. Both groups share a common interest in birds, and both work to preserve and protect them. That one group chooses to do this in the field, while the other chooses the backyard aviary, should be of little concern as long as the birds are not adversely affected. And therein lies the question.

Many exotic species are in real danger of extinction. Part of the reason can certainly be attributed to the pet market that exists for them. The U.S. Fish and Wildlife Service estimates, for example, that in 1982 alone, 800,000 exotic birds were *legally* imported to the United States. Add to that approximately 100,000 that were smuggled. Many received marginal care en route to this country and died during shipment or quarantine.

Many of the countries where exotic birds are natives have taken measures to protect them by prohibiting the exportation of birds. In this country, New York has become the first state to ban the sale of imported wild birds. New Jersey, Massachusetts, and Connecticut are considering similar bills.

The bill, however, should have little effect on bird retailers. Most aviculturists are also cultivation-minded and support the preservation of exotic species. For this reason, most birds offered for sale are captive bred.

The aviculturist breeding large, exotic species has much knowledge to offer concerning avian medicine, maintenance, breeding, and biology. Captive breeding has worked so well for the aviculturist that the same methods are being followed by ornithologists to restore the populations of endangered and threatened species. Cornell University is world famous for its captive breeding and release of peregrine falcons. In California, the California condor, reduced to a *single wild breeding pair* in the early 1980s, has been successfully captive bred. No condors remain in the wild today; all are in the facilities of the Los Angeles Zoo and the San Diego Wild Animal Park. Captive breeding and release programs also are working well on many birds of prey, waterfowl, and pheasants. Exotic finches and canaries sold as aviary pets are exclusively captive bred.

Certainly there are irresponsible hobbyists, just as there are irresponsible birders, and steps should be taken to prevent illegal capture of wild birds. But the aviculturist must not be blamed as the sole cause of a species' decline in its natural habitat. Indeed, the aviculturist may very well be the only way certain species will survive at all, for there are far more serious dangers in the home jungles than a few poachers. . . .

During the 1960s, ornithologists exploring remote areas of Peru made some surprising—and exciting—discoveries. A Princeton biologist named John Terborgh located the Apurimac Valley, some 200 miles due east of Lima. There he found a vast, truly unspoiled rain forest, the watershed of the Amazon, populated by fewer than 2,000 natives. For several years, Terborgh explored the Apurimac, discovering many species of wildlife previously unknown to science, among them "new" owls, wrens, and tanagers.

About the same time, another young ornithologist, John O'Neill, began collecting avian species in the Andes for the Museum of Natural Science at Louisiana State University. Among the birds collected, O'Neill and his colleagues discovered a new species of tanager. Succeeding expeditions to the Andes, the Ecuadorian border region, and the borders of Bolivia yielded more unknown birds.

Needless to say, ornithologists were excited over the discovery of new birds, just when they were beginning to think they had found them all and were concentrating their efforts on the how and why of avian life, rather than the what and where. Biologists began to think differently about remote, unexplored regions of the globe. After all, almost half of the world's avian species are found in the Amazon region. Certainly there must be other new species tucked away in

Deforestation of tropical rain forests is a major factor in the decline of exotic species.

these secret places. But perhaps we will never have the chance to find out.

By the early 1980s, Terborgh's Apurimac paradise had been stripped of vegetation, and some 200,000 people were living there. Similar, uncontrolled destruction has transformed millions of acres of virgin forest into the Amazon Highway. Farmers in Central and South America have leveled more than half of the natural vegetation in their quest for pasture and croplands. And in Carajas, Brazil, the world's largest open-pit iron-ore mine is reshaping the face of the jungle. The government-controlled mining company is building towns, shopping centers, homes, and schools in the southeastern portion of the Amazon basin. A jet-port and a railroad complete the environmentally bleak picture. What other species may have been lost—even before they were found?

The effects of the rapid and widespread destruction of tropical forests is not confined to the "lost" species that may have lived there. The effects are being felt much closer to home, as populations of North American birds that winter in the tropics decline. More than one-third of our breeding birds winter in tropical forests, and various breeding bird surveys and censuses indicate a downward trend in their numbers.

Considering this, it seems that captive breeding and reintroduction programs are terrific, but where will these birds be released if the tropical forests they call home are destroyed? In a short time, it may very well be that the only amazon parrots, macaws, cockatoos, and other exotics in existence are the ones in the aviaries of the aviculturist—like the condors in the California zoos.

AVICULTURE ORGANIZATIONS

If you are interested in the subject of aviculture, there are two organizations that can provide you with information.

The International Foundation for the Conservation of Birds (IFCB) is an organization aimed at uniting aviculturists, ornithologists, veterinarians, government personnel, hobbyists, zoologists, and anyone else interested in the preservation of birds, with emphasis on the captive propagation of endangered species.

The organization regularly provides financial support to individuals and groups of researchers involved in many aspects of field and captive breeding research programs throughout the world. A few of the programs made possible by grants from the IFCB include the Wild Animal Park Greenhouse, a facility used for the propagation of browse plant species for the Zoological Society of San Diego's exotic animal collection; enclosures and breeding facilities at the Summit Zoo, Panama, for the endangered harpy eagle; and funding for England's Wildfowl Trust's construction of an aviary that simulates the natural environment of the torrent duck, a prerequisite for successful captive breeding.

A survey conducted in 1982 cataloged the information on captive-bred birds in 123 major zoos and private collections. The data, representing ninety-two pages of condensed information, were made available to all who participated in the survey. Two of the most notable contributions of the organization were a grant that aided in the construction and maintenance of San Diego Zoo's Avian Propagation Center, and the organization of the IFCB Symposium for breeding birds in

The survival of many species depends on the preservation of specialized habitats.

captivity, which brought together representatives from more than thirty countries around the world.

For more information, write the IFCB at 11300 Weddington Street, North Hollywood, CA 91601.

The American Federation of Aviculture (P.O. Box 1568, Redondo Beach, CA 90278) is a nonprofit organization dedicated to the conservation of birdlife through the use of captive-breeding programs, education, scientific research, and legislative monitoring, with member clubs throughout the United States. The organization publishes *The A.F.A. Watchbird*, which has earned the reputation as being one of the best avicultural magazines in the world. Feature articles on breeding, health, food requirements, hand-rearing young, as well as specialized articles on various species, including wild birds in their natural habitats, are well written and informative. Advertisers offer a wealth of information and supplies.

SEVEN

COOPERATIVE RESEARCH
ORGANIZATIONS AND REFERENCES

Cooperative Research Organizations and References

———

The following directory of environmental groups, information centers, projects, and amateur/professional ornithological organizations will be helpful to you in your birding activities. Contact them for information about their activities, membership, publications, and professional journals.

ORNITHOLOGICAL ORGANIZATIONS

Cornell University Laboratory of Ornithology
159 Sapsucker Woods Road
Ithaca, NY 14850

This facility is a household word among serious birders the world over, who refer to it simply as "Cornell." It needs no other explanation. Founded in 1957, it became the first research laboratory in the United States formed expressly for the study and appreciation of living birds. Cornell strives to bridge the gap between "professional" and "amateur" ornithologists and offers the serious birder more programs, opportunities, contacts, support, encouragement, resources, and results than any other facility of its kind.

In addition to the North American Nest Record Program mentioned earlier, Cornell sponsors a myriad of ornithological projects. A sampling of major ones are:

Seatuck Research Program—Researchers are studying the effects of urban development on wildlife species.

Library of Natural Sounds—Also world famous, as the undisputed leader in researching and recording bird sounds. The collection consists of more than 45,000 recordings of more than 4,000 species worldwide.

Bird Navigation—Using pigeons, Cornell is pioneering research to determine how birds navigate.

Cornell also offers home-study "Seminars on Ornithology" courses that are world famous for their quality. These are college-level course correspondence programs available to anyone. A Cornell instructor works closely with the student. Upon completion students receive a certificate acknowledging their participation in the seminar. They are:

A Home Study Course in Bird Biology—Composed of 301 pages of generously illustrated text, covering all aspects of avian biology, ecology, and behavior. You will learn about the dynamics of flight, the structure and workings of the internal bird, the intricacies of bird behavior, breeding, and rearing of young.

Lessons are sent in installments, at your own pace. As you finish assignments and return them by mail to the lab, the next lesson plan is mailed to you. A Cornell instructor is always available to answer specific questions along the way.

A Home Study Course in Bird Photography—The mechanics of this course are the same as the one above. Through it you will learn how to select and use equipment; how to photograph birds at feeding stations, at nests, and in flight; how to construct and use blinds; how to use motion-picture equipment; and where to sell your photographs.

The Crow's Nest Bookshop offers probably the widest selection of books, recordings, slides, T-shirts, gifts, birding equipment, and related items ever assembled in one place. Catalogs are sent to all members, or upon request.

Membership in the Laboratory of Ornithology includes *The Living Bird Quarterly,* periodical bulletins, and announcements of upcoming field trips around the world.

American Birding Association
P.O. Box 6599
Colorado Springs, CO 80934

The ABA is an organization dedicated to birding as a sport and working toward developing the field expertise of its membership. Publishes *Birding* magazine.

American Ornithologists' Union
National Museum of Natural History
Smithsonian Institution
Washington, D.C. 20560

Organization of professional ornithologists and serious amateurs. Responsible for the AOU Checklist of North American Birds.

Journal: *The Auk*

Cooper Ornithological Society
c/o Berkeley Museum of Vertebrate Zoology
University of California
Berkeley, CA 94720

Organization of professional ornithologists and serious amateurs.

Journal: *The Condor*

Wilson Ornithological Society
c/o Museum of Zoology
University of Michigan
Ann Arbor, MI 48104

Organization of professional ornithologists and serious amateurs.

Journal: *The Wilson Bulletin*

The following organizations are concerned primarily with specific species or families of birds:

Ducks Unlimited
One Waterfowl Way
Long Grove, IL 60047

Eagle Valley Environmentalists, Inc.
Box 155, 112 Stagecoach Road
Apple River, IL 61001

Hawk Migration Association of North America
254 Arlington Street
Medford, MA 02155

National Wild Turkey Federation
Wild Turkey Building
P.O. Box 530
Edgefield, SC 29824

North American Bluebird Society
P.O. Box 6295
Silver Spring, MD 20906

Pacific Seabird Group
Box 321
Bolinas, CA 94924

Peregrine Fund
5666 West Flying Hawk Lane
Boise, ID 83709

Prairie Grouse Technical Council
832 East Sixth Avenue
Emporia, KS 66801

Quail Unlimited
P.O. Box 10041
Augusta, GA 30903

Ruffed Grouse Society
1400 Lee Drive
Coraopolis, PA 15108

Whooping Crane Conservation Association
3000 Meadowlark Drive
Sierra Vista, AZ 85635

ENVIRONMENTAL RESEARCH/CONSERVATION ORGANIZATIONS

Association of Interpretive Naturalists
6700 Needwood Road
Derwood, MD 20855

Audubon Naturalist Society of the Central United States
8940 Jones Mill Road
Chevy Chase, MD 20815

Brooks Bird Club
707 Warwood Avenue
Wheeling, WV 26003

Cousteau Society
930 West 21st Street
Norfolk, VA 23517

Craighead Environmental Research Institute
Box 156
Moose, WY 83012

Earthwatch
680 Mount Auburn Street, Box 403
Watertown, MA 02272

Felicidades Wildlife Foundation
Box 490
Waynesville, NC 28786

Fish and Wildlife Reference Center
3840 York Street, Unit 1
Denver, CO 80205

International Bird Rescue Research Center
Aquatic Park
Berkeley, CA 94710

John Muir Institute for Environmental Studies
743 Wilson Street
Napa, CA 94559

National Wildlife Refuge Association
P.O. Box 124
Winona, MN 55987

Nature Conservancy
Suite 800
1800 North Kent Street
Arlington, VA 22209

Wetlands for Wildlife
39710 Mary Lane
Oconomowoc, WI 53066

World Wildlife Fund
1601 Connecticut Avenue, N.W.
Washington, D.C. 20009

RECOMMENDED READING

CHAPTER 1: A good collection of field guides is standard equipment for the amateur naturalist. Among my favorites are the classic Eastern and Western editions of *Field Guide to the Birds of North America* by Roger Tory Peterson (Houghton Mifflin). I also recommend *The Audubon Society Master Guide to Birding*, in three volumes, edited by John Farrand, Jr. (Knopf); *A Field Guide to the Birds of North America* (National Geographic Society); and *Birds of North America*, by Chandler Robbins, Bertel Brunn, and Herbert Zim (Golden Press).

The Birder's Handbook: A Field Guide to the Natural History of North American Birds, by Paul Ehrlich, David Dobkin, and Darryl Wheye (Simon and Schuster), is an information-packed volume that serves as a nice companion and cross-reference for any collection of field guides.

For learning to recognize bird sounds, listen to *A Field Guide to Bird Songs of Eastern and Central North America*, based on the Peterson field guide series. It is available as an LP record or cassette tapes through the Cornell Laboratory of Ornithology.

Two of the best books on bird feeding are *A Complete Guide to Birdfeeding* and *Beyond the Bird Feeder*, both by John V. Dennis (Knopf). *Welcome the Birds to Your Home*, by Jane P. and Will Curtis (Stephen Greene, Brattleboro, Vermont), and *The Country Journal Book of Birding and Bird Attraction*, by Alan Pistorius (Norton) are also good reading.

The Audubon Society has a five-volume series of home videocassettes, *Audubon Society's Videoguide to Birds of North America*, featuring Roger Tory Peterson and released through the Easton Press in Norwalk, Connecticut.

CHAPTER 2: For subject matter addressed in this chapter I recommend *Manual for the Identification of the Birds of Minnesota and Neighboring States*, by Thomas Roberts (University of Minnesota Press), and *Introduction to Bird Banding Techniques*, by Fred Schaeffer (the Eastern Bird Banding Association).

Other helpful books include *Bird Watcher's Guide to Wildlife Sanctuaries*, by Jessie Kitching (Arco), and *Guide to National Wildlife Refuges*, by Laura and William Riley (Doubleday).

CHAPTER 3: *The Atlas of Breeding Birds in Britain and Ireland*, by J. T. R. Sharrock (A. D. Poyser, Hertfordshire, England), is the text on the original atlas project. As more projects are completed in this country, the published results will become available. Currently, *The Atlas of Breeding Birds in*

New York State, edited by Robert Anderly and Janet R. Carroll (Cornell University Press), and *The Atlas of Breeding Birds of Vermont*, by Sarah Laughlin and Douglas Kibbe (University Press of New England, Hanover, New Hampshire), are readily available.

Also recommended are the series of Stokes Nature Guides, especially *A Guide To Bird Behavior, Vol. I and II*, by Don and Lillian Stokes, and available from Stokes Nature Company in Carlisle, Massachusetts.

CHAPTER 4: The twenty-one volumes of Arthur Cleveland Bent's life histories of different bird families are classics that are entertaining as well as informative. Each volume is titled according to the family group. Among the most useful in my personal collection are *Life Histories of North American Wood Warblers*, in two volumes; and *Life Histories of North American Birds of Prey*, also in two volumes. *Life Histories of North American Birds* are available through Dover Publications in New York.

I also recommend *A Practical Guide for the Amateur Naturalist*, by Gerald Durrell (Knopf); *The Wildlife Observer's Guidebook*, by Charles Roth (Prentice-Hall); and *Thoreau's Method: A Handbook for Nature Study* by David Pepi (Prentice-Hall).

CHAPTER 5: The wildlife rehabilitator can never have enough references! Among the most helpful volumes are *First Aid and Care of Wild Birds*, by J. E. Cooper and J. T. Eley (David N. Charles, North Pomfret, Vermont); *Care of the Wild Feathered and Furred*, by Mae Hickman and Maxine Guy (Unity Press, Santa Cruz); *Care and Rehabilitation of Injured Owls*, by Katherine McKeever (W. F. Rannie, Ontario); and *Wild Orphan Babies*, by William Weber, D.V.M. (Holt, Rinehart & Winston).

One of the most complete references is *Introduction to Wildlife Rehabilitation*, compiled by Adele T. Evans and published by the National Wildlife Rehabilitators Association (RR 1, Box 125E, Brighton, IL 62012). Selected papers, technical reports, notices of wildlife internships, and many additional services are available through this organization.

CHAPTER 6: There are many fine books on the subject of aviculture and the individual species of aviary birds. Among the most helpful publications are "Birdtalk," a monthly magazine published by Fancy Publications (P.O. Box 6050, Mission Viejo, CA 92690). This magazine contains informative articles on basic care, feeding and housing requirements, training, health, breeding and rearing of young, potential problems and cures, behavior, and many more areas of interest. The magazine also features articles and news updates on wild bird management, conservation, and protection of endangered species.

Also recommended are *Parrots and Related Birds*, by Henry J. Bates and Robert Busenbark (T. F. H., Neptune, New Jersey) and *Starting an Aviary*, by Matthew Vriends (T. F. H.).

Many of the organizations listed elsewhere in this book publish newsletters or journals that may be of interest to you. Your local library can also provide a wealth of information about available publications, organizations, and resources.

NEW AGE BIRDING

In addition to the birder's equipment standbys discussed previously in this book—binoculars, scopes, notebooks, journals, and so on—birders can also take advantage of the personal computer. A computer can sort a birder's scrambled field notes into an orderly and easily accessible record that can be quickly updated, rearranged, and analyzed. It can also serve as a springboard for new ideas as to *how* certain data should be considered.

A Field Guide to Personal Computers for Bird Watchers and Other Naturalists, by Edward M. Mair (Prentice-Hall) will tell you everything you will need to know on the subject. Although it was published in 1985, it still is a very useful book.

The book is arranged as a field guide to computers, discussing the evolution and taxonomy of computers, the anatomy, physiology, and topography of your PC, which explains all about hardware, software, printers, bits and bytes, and so forth. The book then discusses behavior—the programs you can choose and how to use them with your birding habit.

For any naturalist involved in serious study, or for the avid birder with volumes of notes, a personal computer can certainly present new possibilities for asking questions and getting anwers. For anyone considering the purchase or use of a computer, this book should be your first step.

As mentioned earlier, the Banding Laboratory has long been using computers to store and analyze their data. In fact, most studies conducted by the Fish and Wildlife Service are done with the aid of computers, as are many of the atlas projects. With the proper equipment, it is possible for the private naturalist and birder to access by telephone information stored in computer data bases anywhere in the world.

More recently, the Fish and Wildlife Service has teamed its CRTs with satellite tracking and transmissions. The Telonics Corporation has designed satellite transmitters to fit an assortment of animals, from humpback whales to polar bears to Canada geese. The transmitters are being used extensively in Alaska to monitor wildlife that is otherwise difficult and dangerous to track. Two weather satellites, orbiting some 510 miles from earth, are able to chart an animal's movements with surprising accuracy and detail, while the biologist receives and reads the information via computer.

For instance, a radio-collared caribou on the Alaskan tundra can be monitored by a biologist 400 miles away in the comfort of a Fairbanks office. Not only does the biologist know *where* the caribou is, but the satellite transmissions are such that its location can be pinpointed within 1,600 feet. The biologist can also determine whether the animal is standing up or lying down, running or walking. A thermometer in the transmitter relays the outside temperature, and a motion detecter tells him in what direction and how often the caribou moves its head.

The satellite tracking system has been used to monitor the migrations of Alaskan wildlife across the Yukon Territory; to track African elephants through hostile countries from the safety of a neutral office; and has followed the movements of whales in the Pacific.

The amount of data that can be obtained using satellites and computers is mind-boggling, and as the method is perfected we will no doubt be hearing more about this fantastic technique and learning much from the information it will bring.

I only hope that, however advanced we become with our technology, we are still able to take the time to walk in the outdoors, with only our own senses, and blend.

Index

precocial birds
    definition of, 115–16
    special care for, 129
returning young bird to nest, 113

ABOUT THE AUTHOR

Laura O'Biso Socha is a self-taught naturalist and writer. She spent most of her childhood and teenage years observing nature and wildlife while roaming the unspoiled lands of the family farm in rural northwestern New Jersey. Her interest in birds led her to the Raccoon Ridge Bird Observatory, where she received training in bird banding and wildlife rehabilitation.

O'Biso Socha lives in Branchville, not far from her childhood home. Her wildlife articles appear regularly in the *Jersey Voice Newsmagazine*. She is currently at work on her second book.